THE DIRECT MAIL SOLUTION

A BUSINESS OWNER'S GUIDE TO BUILDING A

LEAD-GENERATING

sales-driving

MONEY-MAKING

DIRECT-MAIL CAMPAIGN

CRAIG SIMPSON & DAN S. KENNEDY

EP
Entrepreneur
PRESS®

Publisher: Entrepreneur Press
Cover Design: Andrew Welyczko
Production and Composition: Eliot House Productions

This publication is designed to provide accurate and authoritative information
in regard to the subject matter covered. It is sold with the understanding that the
publisher is not engaged in rendering legal, accounting, or other professional services. If legal advice or other expert assistance is required, the services of a compe-
tent professional person should be sought.

Library of Congress Cataloging-in-Publication Data
Simpson, Craig.
    The direct-mail solution: a business owner's guide to building a
  lead-generating, sales-driving, money-making direct-mail campaign / by
  Craig Simpson with Dan S. Kennedy.
      p.   cm.
    ISBN-10: 1-59918-518-0 (pbk.)
    ISBN-13: 978-1-59918-518-7 (pbk.)
      1. Direct marketing. I. Kennedy, Dan S. II. Title.
  HF5415.126.S563 2014
  658.8′72—dc23   2013037976

Printed in the United States of America

18 17 16 15 14   10 9 8 7 6 5 4 3

Contents

Acknowledgments

THANKS TO DAN KENNEDY FOR HIS GUIDANCE, RELENTLESS innovation, instruction, and brilliant insights on marketing and running a business. Without Dan, this book would not have been possible.

Much appreciation goes to my family for supporting me in the penning of this book. Thank you Heidi, Aiden, Quinton, and Ziann!

I also want to say a huge thank you to Ellen Dickstein, my personal friend and editor. She spent hours and hours helping me take my knowledge of direct mail and turn it into *The Direct-Mail Solution.*

It has also been a pleasure to work with Jillian McTigue, director of Entrepreneur Press, and Roe D'Angelo, who provided outstanding editorial feedback. Last, but not least, thanks to Jeff Herman, my literary agent.

How I Started Making Money in Direct Mail—and How You Can, Too!

S A BUSINESS OWNER, ONE OF YOUR PRIMARY GOALS IS TO SEE your business grow and become more profitable. In my experience, direct mail is one of the most powerful tools available to help you achieve that.

Regardless of what business you are in, or how big it is, or even what type of customers you have . . . with the right information, I believe you will be able to develop a direct-mail program that will work for your business.

Marketing is a critical need of every business. It doesn't matter if you are selling software, clothing, or books, or if you manufacture some kind of widget.

Maybe you produce the best face cream in the world. Perhaps it even has the power to rejuvenate the skin and make people look 20 years younger!

You still could end up not making a dime.

That's because unless somebody buys your face cream, you have no income stream. The product is just the beginning of the process. You have to have customers, too.

There's one main way to grow any business, and that's to grow and expand your customer base. It's all about finding new customers and making additional sales to the ones you already have.

You have to find some way to get the word out about your business so that it reaches the widest possible group of potential buyers and convinces them to give you a try.

What are some of your options?

You could hang a sign out in front of your business. That could lure people in, but you would be reaching only the people who happen to be walking down the street and passing by the sign.

You could put an ad in a newspaper, but then you're reaching only people who read that paper, who happen to notice your ad as they turn to the sports section.

You could hire a blimp to carry your message across the sky on a streamer. That could potentially reach the whole city—but only the people who are looking up when the blimp goes by.

But what if you could get your message directly into the hands of large numbers of people—people who are highly qualified to become your customers because they have spent money on products like yours in the past and are likely to spend more in the future?

Even better, what if you could put your message in an attractive package that gets their attention and holds it while you explain all the reasons why your product or service is better than any your competitors can provide?

And what if you could tell them about a special offer that's available for a limited time so that they feel compelled to respond to it immediately?

In a way, it would be as if you were having a private conversation with a thousand, ten thousand, maybe even a million "hot prospects," explaining to them your product, touting its advantages, and presenting your unbeatable offer.

Oh, and one more thing . . . you could have that "private conversation" with people all over the country at the same time.

In essence, that's what direct-mail marketing is all about—reaching out to large numbers of individuals or companies with a targeted, carefully crafted message that you put right in their hands.

And it works! Direct mail has been proven to be an extremely effective way to build and maintain just about any kind of business. In fact, many multimillion-dollar businesses have started with little more than an idea and a sales piece.

Now you too can begin to take advantage of this premier approach to advertising to build your own business. You just have to learn the proven techniques that can make your cash register ring. And I've outlined them for you here in the pages of this book.

My Life in Direct-Mail Marketing

I've spent my entire adult life in the direct-mail field. Over the years I've strategized and executed thousands of direct-mail campaigns. I've seen companies make hundreds of millions of dollars as a result of meticulously planned mailings.

And the techniques that worked for them can do wonders for you. Whether you want to mail only 500 pieces or you're ready to run a nationwide campaign of 100,000,000 pieces—I've done it all. And this book will teach you all the secrets of direct-mail success I've gathered over the years.

But let me start at the beginning. My first experience with direct mail came when I was just 19 years old. I was a young entrepreneur with big dreams, manufacturing rock-climbing holds (the fake rocks you bolt onto a wall to practice rock climbing). My "manufacturing facility" was a small workshop in my parents' garage.

I was selling hundreds of these fake rocks through my friends, but I had big dreams. I wanted to get them into retail shops.

So I bought a list of 100 stores that I thought were good prospects to carry my rocks. Then I wrote a one-page sales letter and stuffed it into an envelope with one of my brochures. After licking the stamps and dropping the mail off at the post office, I sat back, waiting for the phone to start ringing off the hook.

So how did my first campaign do?

It completely bombed—not a single phone call! How could things have gone so wrong? Needless to say, I was extremely disappointed.

And so my first experience with direct mail was similar to that of so many others: an unsuccessful campaign. For a while I even believed as many others do: that direct mail just doesn't work.

Now that I've sent out hundreds of millions of sales letters and generated countless leads and customers, I can look back on my first campaign and laugh. Knowing what I do now, it's obvious to me that I did everything wrong.

First, I got the list of names I mailed to from an unreliable source. So I could have sent my sales piece to people with no interest in rock climbing. Or the names could have been so old that the addresses were no good any more. Second, knowing nothing about writing sales copy, I prepared a very short letter, deluding myself into thinking I could convince people to buy $150 worth of rocks in just two paragraphs. And those two paragraphs were just bad, focusing on the features of my rocks, not on their benefits. (I'll explain more about that in Chapter 2.)

Fortunately, that wasn't the end of the story for me. I didn't give up on my direct-mail campaigns for my rock-climbing-hold business. I kept testing different methods until I found a few that worked. And as a result, I ended up selling over 4,000 fake rocks!

Now, you may be familiar with the saying, "Be careful what you wish for." Success doesn't always turn out to be what we expect, and after a few years of working in my own sweatshop, I decided that manufacturing rocks was not the business I wanted to be in after all.

So I got a job working for a large financial publishing company that had been built upon a highly creative and successful marketing program.

This was my opportunity to learn a lot more about direct-mail marketing and see firsthand how a company could use it correctly to gross over $100 million.

I've been immersed in direct-mail marketing for over 15 years now and have worked with a huge variety of clients in many different business niches. I've sold everything from courses on the benefits of drinking eight glasses of water a day and how to train your bird to do tricks, to technical software, real estate investments, financial investments, continuing-education courses, health products, diet programs, medical professionals, and even wholesale clothing. Just about anything you can think of can be profitably sold through the mail.

I made some mistakes along the way—especially at the beginning. But I learned from all of them, and soon I was helping companies grow from small start-ups to multimillion-dollar businesses through the direct-mail campaigns I ran for them.

I've created this in-depth guide to help save you from making the same mistakes that I made and to show you the techniques I use every day to generate millions of paying customers and countless qualified prospects for my clients.

Direct-mail marketing works for just about any business area. Whether you are a small-business owner, an information marketer, a software developer, or a small retail business owner . . . whether you have an auto-mechanic shop, own an insurance business, run a beauty salon, or even if you just know you want to get into business but you don't know what it is yet . . . whatever it is that you do or want to do, learning the strategies of direct mail will help you be more effective and profitable with your marketing efforts. I'm going to show you how direct mail can be used for any market . . . in any business . . . and in any economy.

To get started, I want to give you a few examples of market niches in which I've seen direct mail work extremely well.

The first is the publishing business. Over the years I have worked for a number of different publishers. The largest was a financial publisher that sold over 700,000 financial educational courses for $195 each (do the math on that one!).

The largest mailing I ever sent was for this publisher—tipping the scales at just over 5.7 million pieces! A paper mill in the state of Washington had to ship 36 boxcars of paper down to Los Angeles where my commercial printer was located . . . just for this one mailing.

In addition to his flagship product, this publisher sold a variety of books, courses, and newsletters. There were years where this business generated over $100 million in sales—and 95 percent of the revenue was initiated through direct-mail campaigns.

I've used this same type of direct-mail marketing to sell information for a real estate information marketer. If you have never explored information marketing or the amount of money you can make with it, you should! A real estate client of mine made over $100 million in one year, and then did it over again in multiple years.

I used the exact same direct-mail marketing methods that I used to sell millions of financial courses and information on real estate to promote a clothing wholesaler. The mailings worked so well for this business that I was mailing out over 50,000 pieces every other week! All based around selling clothing!

I've worked with clients in just about every niche you can imagine, and most of them developed highly successful and very profitable companies that make millions each year, all through the right use of direct-mail marketing.

You May Have Heard . . .

There's a lot of talk you may have heard that the United States Postal Service is in trouble and snail mail is a thing of the past. I'd like to address this issue before we go any further.

Yes, the USPS has some big issues and problems to deal with, but they are not going anywhere. They are here to stay!

The fact is, direct mail is alive and booming, even in today's economic downtrend. The Postal Service is seeing a 5.8 percent increase in the amount of money being spent on direct mail. A whopping $17.8 billion was spent on direct-mail advertising in 2011. The numbers were predicted to be larger than that in 2012. Studies indicate that consumers received 5 billion pieces of direct mail in 2011, compared to 3.6 billion in 2010. The 2012 numbers were expected to show another large increase!

SourceLink, a top marketing agency, reported in 2012 that nine out of ten of their clients named direct mail the medium that was best equipped to help them reach their marketing objectives. In March 2013, Target Marketing's Seventh Annual Media Usage Forecast survey of B2C U.S. marketers reported that the marketing channel that delivers the best ROI for customer acquisition and retention is direct mail.

And these findings work across generations. With all the talk of using email or social networking for marketing, a national survey by ICOM found that in the 18- to 34-year-old demographic, direct mail was the preferred way to learn about marketing offers.

And people love receiving mail. Epsilon surveyed nearly 5,000 customers and found that "U.S. consumers report an emotional boost from receiving direct mail, with 60 percent agreeing they 'enjoy checking the mail box for postal mail.'" People have a great connection with mail. It's personal, tangible, and, if done right, can be highly targeted to individuals' specific interests. The Epsilon survey also revealed that people reported that information received through postal mail was "more trustworthy" than information received through other channels.

And even neuroscience backs up these findings. Using functional Magnetic Resonance Imagery (fMRI) scanning to study brain response, researchers at Bangor University in Wales found that "greater emotional processing is facilitated by the physical material than by the virtual. The 'real' experience that the physical media provides means it's better at becoming part of memory. It generates more emotion, which should help to develop more positive brand associations. The real experience is also internalized, which means the materials have a more personal effect, and therefore should aid motivation."

The bottom line is that this type of advertising really works. Small businesses and entrepreneurs make millions each year from direct mail. Even online businesses use direct mail to drive buyers to their sites, including Google, which uses direct mail to get companies to sign up for their AdWords program. And direct mail can work for your business, too.

Now It's Your Turn

I don't care if your business is small or large. If you take what I'm about to reveal to you in this book and use it, I fully believe that you'll see similar results in your own business. Most won't make $100 million in a year, but I wouldn't be surprised if you increase your business tenfold.

The same strategies work whether you own an auto repair business, have a kitchen supply store, run a publishing company, or sell face cream. It doesn't matter what type of business you are in. Direct-mail marketing can make your business grow!

The following chapters are going to show you—step by step—how to build your business with direct mail. These are the same techniques I've been using successfully for 15 years. You'll learn how to easily acquire new customers and grow your business. And you'll learn how to communicate with your existing customers and get them to give you more repeat business. I've also created a special website for you that includes sample sales pieces, direct-mail reporting examples, gifts, and access to some great resources. You can access it at www. TheDirectMailSolution.com.

Before we proceed, I think it's important to take a moment to introduce marketing guru Dan S. Kennedy, my mentor, friend, and this book's co-author. Dan is a best-selling author, speaker, direct-response marketing consultant, and copywriter who has been creating winning direct-mail campaigns for more than 30 years. His insight and advice makes an invaluable contribution to this book.

And now, on to *The Direct-Mail Solution*. Growing your client base and getting repeat business from your existing customers—this is how direct-mail marketing can turn any business into a gold mine.

—Craig Simpson

How to Think about Direct Mail to Grow Rich

By Dan S. Kennedy

FOR YOU TO REALLY PROFIT FROM THIS BOOK, YOU WILL NEED TO HAVE *faith* and *confidence* in direct mail. You will have to think about it accurately and correctly, be able to justify investment in it and in figuring it out and making it work in your situation. You'll need to be a rational, reasoned believer. How you think about direct mail will predetermine what you will and won't do, how determined and persistent you'll be, and ultimately how successful you'll be with direct mail.

I have produced hundreds of millions of dollars of revenue for myself and my companies, and many hundreds of millions of dollars more of revenue for my clients, over a 40-year term and currently, in over 200 different categories of products, services, businesses, and nonprofits, and I'll share some of those experiences as we go along. But my personal experience is not as important as outright, uncontestable facts.

Facts Are Stubborn Things

It doesn't matter what you think or believe, what others think or believe, what it seems *everybody* thinks or believes. No amount of thinking or believing ever alters fact. It may mask it. But it never alters it. One of the ways you need to think about direct mail is factually. Craig lays out many specific facts. I'll paint in broader strokes.

Many erroneously think of direct mail as outdated and rendered irrelevant by newer media. Others erroneously think of it as too expensive, especially when compared to online media that seems to be free or nearly free, like email. Others think it is too cumbersome and difficult, especially when compared to dashing off a 140-character tweet with one push of one button. But the fact that something is newer, easier to do, or superficially judged cheaper to do is irrelevant. We do not build wealth by any of those things—easier, faster, cheaper, newer. We build wealth with profitable results. Walking is cheaper and easier to do than buying a ticket for a train or navigating preflight security at the airport, but it isn't the most effective or (if your time has value) cost-efficient way to get from Boston to Los Angeles for a meeting. Too often, the way people think about marketing media options is flawed, in two key ways: First, in apples-to-oranges comparisons; second, in terms of raw cost rather than comparative, net return on investment.

The right way to think about direct mail is in the present, its long history notwithstanding. The right way to think about direct mail is in the context of the key marketing question: *How can you best reach, reach out to, and obtain favorable attention from prospective customers, clients, patients, or donors ideally suited to your product, service, business, or charitable cause?* The right way to think about direct mail and to compare direct mail to other media is in the context of true value (never raw cost), considering the quantity and quality of customers delivered, and the net return on investment drawn from total, measured term, or lifetime customer value—a metric Craig discusses in Chapter 8. Finally, the right way to think about direct mail is as a *universally proven* engine of business growth. So if you aren't successfully using it, there's something wrong with you, and you are missing out on key opportunities for growth, profit, and, maybe most important, sustainability and security for your business.

As I'll discuss later, there are lots of media you can use to make sales. None offer as much stability and security to a business as does a direct-mail marketing system that works.

So, despite any chatter and opining you may hear around you from peers, friends, and media, you've made a smart decision stepping into the pages of this book to explore direct-mail opportunities for your business.

The fact is, more commerce is driven and wealth created by direct mail than by any other media. This was true before the internet. It is true now. If direct mail were outlawed on the first day of a month, the economy would grind to a halt by the 30th day of that same month. This truth is supported by the many facts provided to you throughout this book. Even modern media-tech companies like Google rely on direct mail (and telemarketing and human salespeople) to sell advertisers on using their media. Of the top 500 ecommerce sites I know of, nearly all also mail print catalogs, enveloped solo offers and product literature, and postcards, most in large quantities, very frequently. Lifelock, a huge advertiser on radio, in print media, and across the online media spectrum, also mails huge numbers of direct-mail pieces. Companies like J.Crew, with brick-and-mortar stores and robust ecommerce, mail hundreds of millions of catalogs. If you simply look, you will see direct mail playing a role in virtually every kind of business: retail, service, B2C, B2B, and, yes, (supposed) ecommerce. It is not only as I said, a universal and largely essential engine of business growth, it is even more vital in retaining, developing, and selling to existent customers regardless of how they were obtained in the first place.

"Plugging the holes in the money bucket" for businesses, something I do a lot in my consulting practice, always involves direct mail. You can find an in-depth discussion of plugging holes in a business' money bucket in Chapter 5 of my book, *No B.S. Guide to DIRECT Marketing for NON-Direct Marketing Businesses* (2nd Edition), which is an excellent companion to this book narrowed to direct mail.

This is, of course, contrary to the popular perception that direct mail is antiquated, that *everybody* hates "junk mail," that *nobody* reads anymore, that we live in a digital world, and that you, the businessperson, *must* focus on everything online. This statement is also probably contrary to what employees, peers, your trade association and trade journals, the media, friends, and family are all telling you. It is important to listen more to facts than opinions. To methodically follow the money, not popular opinion.

Something has brought you here. A nagging feeling that too much of what you are being pushed to do is laden with waste, defies accountability, is trendy and popular, and is eagerly embraced yet ineffective. An awareness, maybe, that the direct mail you get from very successful companies is clearly built for accountability and must be productive or it wouldn't continue. A desire to be more in control of your sales. Whatever has brought you here, you are going to encounter contrarian facts, strategies, methods, and opportunities. Prepare yourself.

When presented with facts, there are three ways people can react. Ignore them—a popular approach in government. Deny them and insist on contradictory opinions and beliefs. Embrace them and find opportunities by using them.

It is a fact that 1 percent are rich, 4 percent do well financially, 15 percent do okay, and 80 percent are distant, distant also-rans. The Income Pyramid in America, and in virtually any organized sub-population, such as an industry or profession, is a fact. It is not an accident. It is not a forced injustice. There are reasons for this fact, one of which is the way people choose—and they do *choose*—to react to facts.

Prosperity by direct mail is fact. Now we want to find your opportunities to participate and profit.

As an admittedly nonlinear, hop-about introduction to those opportunities, I'll finish off this chapter by telling you about some of my favorite reasons for relying on direct mail for myself and for countless clients, as well as linked entrepreneurial and marketing strategies and sources of power in the marketplace.

The Power of Opposite Direction

In price, there is always a battle, and at the bottom, there is a crowd in combat over cheap, cheaper, cheaper yet, and cheapest. Howard Schultz went in the opposite direction with coffee, and thus we have Starbucks. An enormous amount of price elasticity is available simply by heading in the opposite direction of a crowd.

In distribution, there is always a stampede of followers following followers to any new doorway. J.K. Rowling held her Harry Potter books back and out of digital distribution until millions of copies in hardbound and paperback editions had been sold, thus reaping a much, much, much greater financial harvest from her work. My client, the Guthy-Renker Corporation, created the number-one selling acne remedy, built and then sustained an $800-million-plus business with it (Proactiv®) by *not* putting it on drug store and discount store shelves where *all* the other OTC acne products are.

The entrepreneurial world is full of opposite-direction success stories. A lot of ordinary businesses producing ordinary incomes exist by doing ordinary things. Exceptional businesses producing exceptional incomes tend to go in opposite directions. The entire world of algorithms was birthed by a renegade going in the opposite direction of the entire Wall Street community, a fascinating story told in the first part of the book *Automate This* by Christopher Steiner. Opposite direction is one of the big themes of my *Renegade Millionaire System* and *Renegade Millionaire Marketing System*, a comprehensive blueprint of entrepreneurial fortune-making. (DanKennedy.com/store).

On GKIC stages, we've had a lot of opposite direction entrepreneurs. Gene Simmons of KISS did something no other rock star of his era even imagined—he personally retained all rights to licensing of all the band's images and built and owns one of the largest and richest brand licensing businesses. As Gene says, you can buy KISS-branded condoms and caskets and everything in between. Joan Rivers has made a fortune, building a jewelry business empire not in stores, not by licensing her name, but by selling direct to consumer via the home shopping channel, QVC. I could go on. The point is that, often, acting against common practice and widely held ideas and new, popular fads or trends yields breakthrough outcomes.

The use of direct mail today is its own opposite direction. There is a foolish stampede away from it and, for that matter, away from other "old" media. I have a client in an industry that was badly damaged by direct connection with the real estate and mortgage industry crashes picking up speed from 2008 and 2009 to now. Most of his competitors and peers who survived abandoned all the "old" media they'd relied on and made a complete switch to online media, relying on Google Adwords and manipulated organic search, Facebook advertising and organic search, YouTube, etc., etc., to generate their leads. Even as they saw their lead quantity rise but quality collapse so their costs per sale skyrocketed, they kept pouring all their coal (money+time+attention) into this pit.

My client went in the opposite direction. He just about discontinued his online lead generation and redoubled his use of well-selected mailing lists and direct mail, driving people online to read and watch his video-assisted sales letters and from them to buy his products. He prospered so well at this, he began buying his competitors' customer and unconverted lead lists that they were only willing to email. He mailed them his postcards and multipage sales letters to drive them to his online sales presentations, and he made money with his rivals' lists even though they were losing money marketing to them!

The clutter in mailboxes has, in fact, thinned, a Darwinian thinning of the herd. This is an advantage for today's direct-mail marketers— like my client. As all his competitors congregated online and created overwhelming clutter, confusion, and chaos in peoples' email inboxes and throughout the media they used, like Google and Facebook, he took over the territory they abandoned and, in his category, pretty much had it all to himself.

Direct mail is the rare creature jointly owned by renegade millionaires and, *at the same time*, the well-established giants and leaders and the most profitable small businesses in hundreds and hundreds of categories.

The Power of "Evergreen" and "Autopilot," Predictability, and Reliability

You do not need to be psychic to predict income.

My clients have direct-mail campaigns that I created for them 3, 5, 7, as much as 11 years ago. They mail week in and week out, and have not needed to change one whit. Because of this, they can accurately predict the number of new customers being acquired and the amount of income being created. Further, many lock it all in on autopilot. The chosen lists go the mailing house; the needed quantity of the direct-mail pieces go to the mailing house; a preset number are mailed each week; a predicted number of sales are made each week or a predicted number of appointments are created for a practice, and a predicted number of people come to a store or showroom. Such a direct-mail asset is, inside the industry, called "evergreen," because it does not brown-out or die, nor even need watering, fertilizing, or attention. It is much, much more difficult to achieve evergreen in other media, particularly with online media, where the speed of change, copycatting, and changing of rules by the media itself—for example, Google's incessant changes in algorithms, content requirements, and ranking formulas. Most successful advertising created these days has painfully short shelf life, except in direct mail.

The Power of Showing Up Alone

Consider the purchase of a commodity, say, a mattress or a portable space heater. If you search "mattress" on Google, you'll get a dizzying array of over 100,000 product choices, informational pieces, consumer reports, and other things to look at. If you go to Amazon.com and search, you'll find a myriad of options being sold by Amazon, and by other vendors operating their own stores on Amazon's platform. If you go to a Home Depot store in October and look at space heaters, you'll find an aisle full of different products to pick from. Surrounded by variably priced, seemingly comparable options, 80 percent of all consumers pick from the bottom one-third of the prices. Increasingly, consumers also price-compare what's in front of them on the shelf with other sellers via their smartphones.

Showing up amid a lot of competition cripples price and profit. In such environments, long-established, familiar brand names have advantage, and if you are a lesser-known but superior choice, you are at disadvantage. The internet is not really as democratizing a force in commerce as it is often made out to be. The majority of traffic converted to buyers is bought and paid for, most of it by the highest bidders—not obtained through organic search. And the traffic obtained via "showrooming"—price comparing through smartphone while standing in store—invariably goes to the lowest-price merchant.

If you choose to mud-wrestle in this swamp, I wish you well, but you might be better served, wealthier, and happier by opting out. There is an old line about recessions and No Parking Zones: *They are for everybody else. I refuse to participate.* Some savvy users of direct mail can say the same thing about competition.

There are only two sales channels that actually remove the consumer from competition, clutter, chaos, and confusion and focus him on a yes or no decision, on acceptance or rejection of one offer or provider. One is the salesperson placed in the consumer's home or office, mano-a-mano, face-to-face, nose-to-nose, toes-to-toes. The other is the sales *letter* placed in the consumer's hands, as he sits in his recliner or at his desk. The latter is the closest possible experience to the first.

And only my sales letter can bring my customer directly to my mattress store, predetermined to buy a mattress from me and no one else. Only my sales letter can keep the homeowner out of Home Depot and out of Google and get him to pick up the phone and buy my space heater. With direct mail, you can show up alone and bolt the door behind you when you enter.

The Power of the Full and Best-Told Story

A lot of media imposes a lot of pressure to abbreviate your sales story. Don't.

Personally, I find 30- and 60-second radio and TV commercials the toughest media to work with. Most experts and most consumers insist that 7 minutes, give or take, is the maximum attention that'll be given to online video, although I can point to notable exceptions, where 20-, 40-, 60-minute—or even 4-hour—online video presentations have made and are making millions of dollars. To me, the media offering the least pressure to tell less than the best-told story is direct mail. With different direct-mail formats, I can successfully engage people in very long copy and gain the opportunity I want most: to tell my full and best story without compromise, to prospects picked to receive it because of known interest in it. I have routinely created and mailed 12-, 16-, and 32-page sales letters, 24- to 64-page booklets, and other similarly long copy pieces with audio CD or DVD. If I can make it interesting for an interested prospect, he will read it all, listen to it all, and watch it all.

This is particularly important for the most difficult marketing, selling, or lead-generation tasks—such as presenting complex propositions, new and unfamiliar propositions, things that are met with high levels of skepticism, or premium price products or services. Abbreviating these kinds of sales stories to fit preset limits of inflexible media or to meet short attention spans linked to certain media can be deadly.

The Power of Time Commitment

This is a secret: The more time a prospect invests with a marketer, the more likely he is to buy from him.

In direct sales, for years, the leaders in selling encyclopedias, fire alarms, vacuum cleaners, and water purifiers had sales presentations deliberately engineered to last 90 minutes to 2 hours. They might have been abbreviated, even to the point of allowing each salesman to run three or four appointments per night, rather than one or two. But it was well understood that the longer you stayed in the home, the more likely you were to leave with a sale.

Sales letters are basically salespeople arriving in envelopes instead of on foot. Direct mail affords the best opportunity to interest, somewhat obligate, and engage the prospect for the longest time commitment. With a good direct-mail piece to a well-selected prospect, I may be able to get him to read a 16-page letter, watch a 30-minute DVD, and pop a 60-minute audio CD into his car's player to listen to and from work the next day. It's nearly impossible to secure this time investment with any other form of outreach but direct mail. One of my all-time, most successful sales letters is 64 pages long. A person reading it *is* time invested.

But Wait—There's More!

I've enumerated only a few of many profound advantages of direct mail. You will discover more as you progress through this book.

The industrialist Henry J. Kaiser observed that opportunity usually arrives wearing work clothes—and brings a set of overalls and work boots for you. This book does that. If you are up for it, this work can transform your business and your income.

Direct-Mail Basics and Creating the Perfect Sales Piece

DIRECT MAIL IS ONE OF THE MOST EFFECTIVE METHODS I KNOW TO take a small business and make it grow fast. You can quickly and easily reach out to large numbers of people, telling them all about the great features of your product or service and giving them instructions on exactly what they need to do to start improving their lives with what you have to offer.

Yes, it's true that there are other forms of advertising you can use. But direct-mail marketing offers a huge advantage over most advertising media, and that advantage is that you can use it to target very specific groups of customers or prospects.

Of course, it can also be used to reach a broad range of prospects with your mailings—as broad as you would reach with TV—if that's your wish. Think about those ubiquitous Publisher's Clearinghouse

Sweepstakes mailings. I remember those arriving in the mailbox when I was a kid, and you probably do too. They worked, or they wouldn't still be doing them!

But it's the ability to zero in on your specific audience that makes direct mail so cost effective—especially when you're starting with a specific product or service that won't be of interest to everyone in the world. You want to know your advertising dollars are being used to reach the right people.

With direct mail you can target people by age, sex, income, hobbies, and interests. You can narrow down the people you mail to by what they have bought in the past and how much money they've spent. In other words, you can make your mailing specific to the type of customer you're looking for. This increases the probability that you'll get the response you want.

For example, if you are selling a special golf driver for $400, and you want to mail only to buyers who have spent $400 or more on golf equipment, then you'll be able to identify and then mail to the exact type of prospect you want to reach: individuals who are golfers who have spent $400 or more on golf-related products within the past year.

What other advertising medium allows you to be this specific? Direct mail gives you the option either to mail to a broad universe of prospects or a very specific, targeted, narrowed-down, niche population.

Then you can send a message that's carefully tailored to appeal to the group you're sending to. Targeted sales pieces allow you to grab your prospects' emotions, and then you can motivate them to respond by presenting a special offer.

You can give your prospects the option of responding in many different ways. You can direct prospects to call a phone number, have them come right down to your storefront, visit your web page, mail something back to you, or even send you a fax or email—whatever works best for you and your type of business.

As you can see by now, direct-mail marketing gives you lots of flexibility in the kind of prospects you can reach, the kind of sales material you will send them, and how you will ask them to respond.

But even with all that flexibility, a basic direct-mail campaign always involves these three basic elements:

1. Sending out sales pieces with a targeted message . . .
2. To a select group of people . . .
3. And asking them to do something very specific—a direct call to action that motivates and tells prospects how to respond.

This book is all about designing and running a direct-mail campaign around these three elements. But before you can send something out, you need something to send! You need a great sales piece.

It All Starts with a Sales Piece

In this chapter we'll focus on the sales piece and how to get one that will do the job. With the right sales piece you could see your phone ring off the hook, your mailbox overflow with orders, or your web page receive hundreds or even thousands of hits.

Having an excellent sales piece is a critical part of the success of any campaign. When I first started out in this business, I worked for a man who built a multimillion-dollar company on an unusual sales piece he wrote himself. It worked so well rival companies copied his methods for years.

This man knew how to write a sales piece that appealed to a very deep need in people. I'll never forget something I heard him say again and again about advertising: "It's not the product that's important. It's the sales piece."

Of course, you need a great product, too. You need something to sell! But unless you have an appealing sales piece, you won't be able to sell your product, no matter how wonderful it may be.

Writing an effective sales piece requires a real understanding of the product or service you're selling, and then putting all your enthusiasm

The Sales Piece That Created a Millionaire

Ken Roberts was a young man who was determined to become rich. He tried several different businesses with modest success, and then he discovered commodity trading. A natural-born teacher and motivator, he developed a course to teach the skill to others. And that's when he discovered he was a natural-born copywriter as well.

Ken wrote a sales piece to sell his course that was so effective it set him on the path to the wealth he'd always dreamed of. Over the years he sold so many courses that *Worth* magazine said he taught commodity trading to more people than anyone else on the planet. One feature of this unique sales piece was that he wrote it in the first person, telling his own story, but in such a way that any reader could identify with him and think he could accomplish what Ken did. The copy was many pages long, but because it was so compelling, the reader couldn't put it down. Finally, the piece was published as an attractive booklet, making it fun to read.

There were probably other qualities that made this sales piece work as well as it did. Whatever they were, it was the perfect combination, and it made Ken a millionaire, many times over.

for it into the piece. You want to make your audience as excited about it as you are.

In addition to your knowledge and interest in your product—that only you can bring to the process because nobody knows your product as well as you do—you have to know some simple copywriting techniques that have proved successful over the years. There's no reason why you can't be the one to write the next million-dollar sales piece. (Or at least direct a professional copywriter who will write it for you.)

The following information should help you get started.

AIDA

There's a famous formula for writing excellent sales pieces that has been part of the copywriter's bag of tricks for many years now. It's called the AIDA formula, an acronym for:

A = Gain **A**ttention
I = Create **I**nterest
D = Build **D**esire
A = Request **A**ction

Pick up any sales piece that you like, and analyze it for these four elements. Chances are you'll find that they're all there.

In some way the piece first grabs your attention. It may be with a great headline or a graphic element. Whatever it is, the piece immediately catches your eye, and you can't help but pick it up to find out what it's all about.

Once it has your attention, the piece intrigues you with the promise that something is about to be revealed that will be of benefit to you. Now your interest is aroused. You just have to learn what the big secret is.

Then it builds a desire in you to obtain the product. Often it will do that by showing you that you have a problem (maybe a problem you didn't even know you had until you read the piece) and then offering an easy solution that only the person sending the sales piece can provide.

Finally it will have a very clear call to action: step-by-step instructions for what you have to do in order to get all the benefits you've been promised. A sales piece that doesn't have a clear call to action is almost worthless.

Without all of these elements, a sales piece may not give you the results you want. Before you send out any direct-mailing piece, make sure it at least follows the AIDA formula.

How Long Should a Sales Piece Be?

There is much debate about how long a sales piece should be. I've tested and seen over and over that, in general, the longer the piece, the more success it will have. Once you get the reader interested, you just have to drive your point home with tons of benefits, proof, and convincing arguments. And the more the better.

Possibly you've read somewhere that shorter copy is better—that it is better to just get to the point rather than ramble on with a long letter. Just before I started writing this chapter I talked to a client who said, "I think we just need to tell people what we are selling within the first few paragraphs. No one has time to read through all those words." This was his first reaction to an eight-page sales letter to his existing customers. He only wanted to mail two pages.

I bit my tongue and politely disagreed with him and explained that there is an art to selling. You can't just tell someone to buy something and expect them to buy it. If it was that easy, we'd all be broke from buying everything offered to us.

The fact is, research shows again and again that it's the longer copy that sells. This is especially true for products that people don't really need. People don't need to be convinced to buy things they need, like washing machines or snow tires. When you buy these things, you're happy with a bulleted list of features in a catalog.

But when it comes to things you don't need, and never even thought about before, like a new set of golf clubs or a new miracle diet and exercise program, you need lots of information to convince you— and the more the better.

But now you're thinking, if I have no interest in going on a diet, I'm sure as heck not going to read a 36-page sales piece about it. Well, maybe yes and maybe no. But one thing you can be sure of is that someone who *does* feel like it wouldn't be a bad idea to lose a few pounds might eagerly read every word of the long sales piece. And research—and sales figures—back up the efficacy of longer pieces.

One of my favorite direct-marketing quotes is "the more you tell, the more you sell." I've never seen a direct-mail (physical mail) campaign where a shorter sales letter worked better than a longer sales letter.

My first real direct-marketing job was with one of the most successful financial publishers in the business opportunity niche. I sent out millions of sales pieces for him. We constantly tested, and the results led us to increase the page count. The sales piece we were mailing grew from 56 pages to 64 pages to 72 pages to 80 pages. Each increase in page count increased our response rate.

One of my clients sends out an oversized, 11 x 6-inch PURL postcard each month. (A PURL postcard sends people to their own "Personal URL"—for example, simpson-direct.com/craig.simpson). I convinced him to test a four-page self-mailer because it would include more copy and cost about the same to mail. The results were significantly better. More proof for "the more you tell, the more you sell."

I've tested long and short copy many times, and I've always seen a higher response rate with the longer copy. Now, there are times when the increased printing and production costs offset the higher response. If the longer piece bumps you into a higher postage class, then you'll need a significant lift in response in order to offset the higher price. But 90 percent of the time, you'll find that it's well worth your time and extra cost to increase the length of your copy.

It's also true that many people have had successful campaigns with a two-page letter or even a well-written postcard. Important factors in determining the length of the sales piece are what it is you're selling, how much explanation is required, how much the item costs, how knowledgeable your audience is, what is the call to action, etc. For example, if you have a list of steady customers and you just want to let them know a popular product is on sale, a quick postcard that makes it easy for them to see that information may be the perfect vehicle.

I've directed extremely successful campaigns with sales pieces of every length. I've sent out invitation-style mailers, "newspaper reprint" mailers, four-page self-mailers, digest-size sales pieces that ranged from 16 to 80-plus pages in length, postcards—just about anything you can think of. (We'll be describing all of these formats and when and how to use them later in this book.)

There's a famous story that someone once asked Abraham Lincoln how long a man's legs should be. His answer was, "They ought to be long enough to reach from his body to the ground." That sums it up for me too when it comes to the question of how long a sales piece should be.

One final thought on this topic: whenever I'm working with a copywriter on a sales letter, I never give a specific page count that must be fulfilled. The writer always asks how many pages are needed, and I always answer, whatever it takes to get the job done. When you are writing copy, never set a specific page count you need to achieve. Instead, write what you think will work best. Write as much copy as you think is needed to convince the prospect to respond to your campaign. Don't limit yourself by setting a page count.

The Elements of a Sales Piece

You may be thinking, "How am I going to write a sales piece?" If you've never done anything like that before, it might seem impossible. But let me tell you why you would be the perfect one to write—or at least be the one to consult on the creation of—the sales copy for your business.

- $ *You understand your product or service.* You know its strong points and its weaknesses. You know what makes it unique and better than anything else out there.
- $ *Hopefully, you love your product or service.* You have great enthusiasm for it. You probably think about it every waking hour, and

maybe you even dream about it at night. It is that positive energy that readers pick up on that makes them want to know more about the product and what it can do for them.

$ *You are familiar with your competition.* You know their strengths and weaknesses and why what you offer is a superior product.

$ *You understand your prospects.* You know why they need your product, what problem they have that it can solve for them, what they're looking for specifically, and how your product is designed to meet their need.

$ *You know the story of the product.* How you got involved with it. How it changed your life. How your passion for some idea drove you to create it or get involved with it. Stories make great sales pieces. They grab people's interest and get them hooked so they'll keep reading all the way to the end and finally place the order.

In other words, you are the best resource for all the information that is going to be the basis of your winning sales piece.

And good sales copywriting is often informal and comes from the heart. If you can talk about your product to other people, there's no reason why you can't jot down your ideas and turn them into a written sales piece.

And once you get started, it can actually be fun. Every time you come up with a great idea to add, like a new benefit, and every time you come up with an exciting new way to describe your product, you'll feel like you found a pearl in an oyster. You'll quickly jot it down, and the more you do, the more ideas you'll get.

Then all you have to do is gather together all your notes, and it's just like assembling a jigsaw puzzle. You start putting all the pieces together in the right order, and before you know it, you have a sales piece! Once you have the main pieces stitched together, you just have to polish it up a bit, and you'll be ready to go.

Just start writing down points as they come to you throughout the day. Think of some of your customers who used your product or service and had a good experience so you can throw in some examples. You may already have the makings of a fantastic sales piece inside of you, just waiting to be expressed on paper.

If you're going to try creating your own sales copy, a good way to start is to put together a collection of sales pieces that appeal to you. You probably receive mailings every day from companies. Which ones grab your interest or have a tone that appeals to you? What are the elements of the piece that really capture your interest or make it seem convincing? What is it that clinches the deal for you? Spend some time studying them carefully.

Also, think about the following elements that will influence how you write the piece.

- $ *The message:* What is your product about? What does it do? What makes it special? Why would someone want to buy your product? What's the benefit to them of buying it?
- $ *The audience:* Who will be receiving the sales piece? What are they after? What do they already know and what will you have to explain to them? What do you believe will appeal to them about your product?
- $ *The offer:* What is the specific offer in the sales piece? Are you offering a special price or an added bonus? What will people receive if they order now instead of waiting? It's usually good to have an irresistible offer with a time limit to encourage a quick response. You want them to order NOW! Give them an incentive to do so. And make sure you have a clear call to action—step-by-step instructions for what you want the reader to do next.
- $ *The voice:* Every sales piece has a "voice." It may be a personal voice or an impersonal, expert voice. It may sound like it's coming from the owner of the company, or it may sound like it's coming from a third party. It can sound urgent, scary, encouraging, humorous. It can say "I'm just like you," or "I know how to help you." The more you know about your audience, the better you'll

know what voice to use in the piece. Above all, you want the piece to make you sound believable and trustworthy.

$ *The lingo:* You want the piece to speak the language of your audience. If there are certain buzzwords that should be used or certain specific expressions, use them judiciously; you don't want to overdo it. You can make a list of these words and expressions and refer to it while you're writing. But if you're writing to a general audience who will be put off by buzzwords, don't use them.

In general, if your sales piece makes your potential buyers feel that you are talking directly to them, that you understand their needs, that you have a unique solution to their problems, that you will deliver on what you promise, and that you have a great offer, you will be well on your way to receiving a great response from your sales letter.

Make the Most Out of Every Part of Your Sales Piece

If you were building a model airplane, it wouldn't be any good to make most of it great but to leave off the left wing or connect the rudder upside-down. You would completely undo all your good work by being sloppy in even one area. If the airplane is going to be worth anything at all, every part of it has to be perfect.

It's the same with your sales piece. You want to get the absolute most out of every one of its parts. You don't want to skimp on anything. The success of your business is riding on your piece doing its job. That means you have to do your job and give each section all the attention it deserves.

Every sales piece has exactly the same elements, no matter how long it is. Whether your sales piece is a postcard, a two-page letter, or a 36-page booklet, it will have all or most of the following parts. Make sure you give attention to each one you include.

$ *Headline:* You have to grab your reader's interest in just a few seconds. And the way to do that is with a great headline. It can be just a few words long, or it can be several sentences. But it has to capture interest and make or imply a promise that you are offering something that will be of great value to the reader—and they'd better read the piece right away to find out what it is. Getting the right headline is job one!

$ *Benefits:* The one question every potential buyer is going to ask is, "What is this going to do for me?" So throughout your piece you have to keep piling on the benefits.

And keep in mind that it's benefits, not features, that sell. That new car may have the most advanced engine, but the buyer wants to hear that he'll be able to drive fast and impress the neighbors. That new diet supplement may have an impressive list of ingredients, but the buyer wants to know it will make her husband love her and her friends envy her.

Always stress benefits that will appeal to your audience. If you're selling a money-making opportunity to a novice audience, you would want to stress that it's easy to learn with no experience needed. If your audience is a group of veteran traders, you would want to stress that this is a new and profitable trading technique they've never seen before.

$ *The Offer and Call to Action.* By the time your reader comes to the end of the sales piece there should be no doubt as to what to do next. You want to create a sense of urgency by providing a call to action. As we say in the business, "always ask for the order."

And you want people to act right away. If they put the sales piece down, even if they're interested, they will soon forget. All that enthusiasm you worked so hard to develop will fade out.

To avoid that happening, you can encourage people to act immediately by offering an incentive for buying within a certain time period. It could be a special reduced price, a bonus gift, or any other extra you want to throw in if they will just "act now."

Another way to encourage action is to make it clear how easy it is to respond and that with your toll-free number, they don't have to pay for the call. With today's calling plans, many people don't pay for individual calls anyway, but there's something about a toll-free number that is very appealing. It's a psychological thing.

$ *The PS.* Research shows that one of the most important parts of a sales letter is the PS. Very often people will look at the opening of the piece, and then turn to the back to see what the offer is. If there's a PS there, they'll often read it before anything else.

So make sure you always put an appealing PS that reiterates the most important points of your sales pitch. Remember, you want every part of your piece to work hard for you. Make sure your PS is doing everything it can to clinch the sale.

$ *The Order Form.* If you're using an order form with your piece, this is your last chance to sell your product and convince your prospect to go ahead and make the purchase. Always include brief, attractive copy about the product, its benefits, and the offer.

$ *The Guarantee.* OK, this is optional, but it can be very powerful. Your potential buyer may be very tempted but still afraid to lose money. If you put in a satisfaction guarantee, it can convince prospects sitting on the fence to go ahead and try your product because they "have nothing to lose."

$ *The BRE.* This is also optional. If you would like your prospects to respond by mail, you can consider inserting a Business Reply Envelope (BRE) into your mailing package. The BRE is preaddressed to you, and the prospect does not have to put postage on the envelope (the post office bills you postage for each envelope mailed back to you). By making it easy for your prospect to respond, you may increase response rates.

Again, just as it pays to point out to prospects that they can call using a toll-free number, make sure your prospects know they can send in their order form postage paid. Not only is it free, but they don't have to go to the bother of finding a stamp!

Use all the parts of your sales piece to full advantage. Don't be satisfied with any part of the piece that just "gets by." Put as much care into each aspect of your piece as possible, and it will work hard for you.

Adding Spice to Your Sales Piece

Good copywriting creates exciting pictures in the reader's mind. Here are some easy tricks to producing copy that sells.

Make It Easy to Read

When people pick up a sales piece, they will start by quickly glancing through it. To grab their attention your copy must be interesting, and at the same time it should be easy to read.

- $ Keep paragraphs short.
- $ Don't use convoluted sentence structure.
- $ Use bullet points so they can easily see your main benefits and features.
- $ Keep repeating the main point in different ways. That way the message is sure to sink in.
- $ Guide the reader with subheads that tell a story.

Use Images and Magic Words

Draw pictures of how the reader will feel with that beautiful new car in the driveway or driving it. How they will feel on their luxury vacation and how relaxed they will be. What they will look like with fewer wrinkles and youthful skin. Be specific in the images, but not so specific your readers won't be able to tailor the images with their own fantasies.

Also, certain words are proven to sell: Free, New. Use them wherever you can.

Again, stress benefits, not features. Tell readers how their lives will be improved with your product.

And testimonials can be extremely effective. Presenting proof that other people used the product and benefited from it will be very persuasive to your reader.

Have an Angle

One day you receive two sales pieces in the mail. The headline on one says:

"My Course Will Teach You Everything I Know
About Trading Stocks"

The headline on the other says:

"Learn the Stock Secret I Used to Make Six
Figures in Six Months"

Which piece are you more likely to read? I'll bet it's the second one. Why? Because it has an angle—a clever way of presenting the information that makes it clear what the unique advantage is that the seller has to offer the reader. The first one just says "I'll teach you how to trade stocks." But who am I, and why should you care?

In the second headline the angle is that the information I have to share is "secret," and it made me a sizable amount of money in a short amount of time.

What other angles could you use for this same product?

If you're sending your piece to people with no experience trading stocks but who just want to make money, you might play up the angle that anyone can learn this, even if you've never traded a stock in your life.

Or, let's say you're writing to commodity traders, and you want to convince them to try trading stocks with your method. You might promise them they can enjoy the same returns as they do with commodity trading but with one-fourth the risk.

Or suppose you're writing to a group of people nearing retirement. You know they may be focused on building their nest egg and are worried they may not have enough time to build their account before they stop working. Then you might promise this is the ideal method to fund a retirement account: It works quickly with relative safety.

You need a hook that will get attention and will appeal directly to your target audience. What is it about your product that makes it of special interest and value to them? That's the point you want to stress throughout your piece. That's your angle. With the right angle, everything else about your piece will fall right into place.

Have a Story

Long sales pieces can be great. Long, dull sales pieces can be a complete waste.

Think of it this way. You'll happily read a 300-page mystery novel, but you'll toss aside a one-page legal disclaimer. Above all, to be successful your sales piece has to keep the reader's interest.

When you look through your sales piece, ask yourself, if you found this in your mailbox, would you read it? Yes, you have certain information you have to get across, but if no one will read it, you won't get anything across.

One technique many copywriters use to make a sales piece interesting is to play up "the story." It could be the story of the person who developed the product. Or it could be the story of someone who used the product and whose life was changed as a result. The idea is that the reader identifies with the person in the story, becomes involved enough to keep reading to find out what happened, and comes to the conclusion, "I'm just like that person, and there's no reason I can't have the exact same experience using this product."

People especially love a rags-to-riches story. "I was poor (sick, lonely, etc.). Then I learned this secret, and now I'm healthy, happy, and rich. And now I will share everything I learned with you." Some of the most effective sales pieces ever written have taken exactly that approach.

Only you know your story and how it relates to your product. How you saw a need and worked hard to find a way to fulfill it. How you struggled to arrive at the answer. How you overcame obstacles to reach your goal. How the answer you found was unlike anything anyone has come up with before. This is your opportunity to sell yourself (or whomever created the product). Why are you an expert? Why are you the one to provide the solution to the reader's problem? Often a personal story about the individual who created the product makes for a very compelling sales piece.

Of course, the story isn't really about you. It's about the product and what it will do for the reader. So always bring it around to that. What is it about this product that is so unique and so much better than anything else out there?

If you're writing your own sales piece, now's the time to start thinking about everything that brought you to this moment. And if you're working with a copywriter, it's up to you to be open and share your experience. Give the copywriter the material needed to create a moving, compelling piece that will grab the reader's attention and convince him that you are real, that you are sincere, and that you truly have the solution he is looking for.

Keep Them Guessing

It always helps to add a touch of "intrigue." You want the reader to feel compelled to keep going, wondering what great revelation is coming next.

The copywriter's task is to first get the reader interested and then keep him moving through the piece, all the way to the close. You don't want to lose the reader anywhere along the way. One method writers often use is to keep hinting at what is about to be revealed next, so the reader keeps following the "trail of crumbs." For example, maybe you want to make sure the reader gets through a relatively boring part, so you keep him involved by saying, "I'll tell you about how I had my big breakthrough in a minute, but first I have to give you some background information so you can understand the genius of it . . ."

Another technique is to structure the piece around a series of subheads. The proper use of subheads can act like that "trail of crumbs" and will pull the reader along nicely. Before the reader sits down to read the piece word for word, he or she will likely flip through the piece and read the eye-catching subheads which, by themselves, will tell a story. If that story sounds interesting enough and related enough to the reader's interests and goals, the motivation will be there to read the entire piece.

Don't think your product is too dull or practical to have some intrigue associated with it. How did your construction firm resolve the mystery of the dissolving sheet rock to create a new sealant? How did your natural dry cleaning solution solve the mystery of the itchy sweater?

A Little More About That All-Important Call to Action

I'm constantly amazed at the failure of a marketing message to make a clear call to action. If you don't put a strong call to action in your direct-mail campaign, you are wasting your money. You want to make it abundantly clear what you want your prospect to do.

You may even want to list the call to action more than one time within the sales message. Make it as easy as possible by outlining the steps the prospect needs to follow in order to respond to your offer.

Recently I received a postcard from my local hospital. I'm still scratching my head trying to figure out why they wasted advertising dollars on this direct-mail campaign. Basically the postcard has a picture of two smiling young men. The copy on the card indicates that two new doctors have arrived at the hospital, and they are looking for "consultations and surgical care" patients.

When was the last time you received a postcard from a hospital or surgeon and decided, "Great, I'm so glad I got this reminder. I've always suspected I could benefit from knee surgery. I guess I'll call this new surgeon, who is fresh out of college and has little experience, to schedule my surgery."

Thankfully marketing isn't that easy or else I'd be out of a job.

The thing I find humorous about this postcard is the fact that it's coming from my local hospital. The small town I live in has only one hospital. There is no one else in town to compete with them. If someone in my family is injured and needs immediate medical attention, I only have two choices. I can either drive a few minutes to my local hospital or I can drive 40 minutes to the hospital in a nearby town. Hmmm—what should I do? I know, it's an emergency, so I guess I should go to the nearest hospital. Wow—that's brilliant!

The hospital could have done a much better job spending its advertising dollars.

- Instead of mailing to everyone in town, it should have narrowed its list down to those who are older and more likely to need surgery. Or, even better, they could have rented a list of names and addresses featuring people who have filled out a survey and specifically noted they have an ailment of some sort.

- The hospital should have told the story of the new doctors. As far as I can tell, they are fresh out of college with no experience. Who knows? Maybe they just look young, but they are actually super experienced and have done thousands of procedures. The hospital needs to tell us why we should have confidence in these new doctors. If they are fresh out of school, they could say something like, "Dr. Martin has just finished studying the latest procedures for modern medicine. He is one of only 30 doctors who are certified to use XYZ Method, which shortens the recovery time for most patients. He has two young kids and picked Grants Pass as the perfect place to raise his family . . ."

- It should have used a legitimate call to action. No one is going to schedule a consultation from the postcard it sent me. There are many different calls to action it could have used. It could have offered a free report, "7 Things You Should Know Before Having Surgery." Or, it could have hosted a reception to meet the doctors and listen to a short presentation on "7 Things You Should Know Before Having Surgery." Or, "Call for a FREE consultation to determine if surgery is right for you!"

I could list more options and suggestions for a better direct-mail promotion, but I'll stop with just those three. In the end, the postcard failed because it didn't contain a legitimate call to action that is motivated by strong copy.

Always Write to an Audience of One

One mistake I see copywriters make again and again is that they write to some nameless, faceless audience. They think of "prospects"—in the plural—rather than about individual buyers.

If you get a letter that opens with a salutation like "To Fly Fishermen Everywhere," you can be pretty sure the writer was not approaching the job with the correct mind-set. If I see "To Fly Fishermen Everywhere," I'm not personally engaged. I don't like being lumped into big groups. I figure the writer just wants to sell as many of his gizmos as he can, and he doesn't know anything about me and my personal needs.

But if I get a letter that opens, "Dear Craig, I know you enjoy fly fishing like I do . . ." it feels a little more personal, and I'm more likely to want to read whatever follows. (And with today's printing technology, it's easy to personalize pieces in this way.)

It's the copywriter's task to make the reader believe that this letter is coming directly from another human being right to him or her. We all want to feel that we are recognized as individuals—even if it's only in a sales letter that we sense is going to thousands of other people. At least we want the illusion that the material in this letter is meant to fulfill our personal need.

And it's important that the copywriter have this mind-set, too, because this is the key to writing compelling copy that answers the needs of the reader. The writer must put himself in the reader's place and ask, "What would I want to know that would convince me that this is the product for me? That it would be worth it to me to spend my hard-earned money on this product?"

Some of the best copywriters I know tell me that they always only write to one person. They'll picture that person in their mind, sitting across from them at a kitchen table, listening to what they have to say. Groups don't buy your products. Individuals do. And you have to write to individuals.

What If You Don't Want to Write Your Own Sales Piece?

Okay, maybe becoming a writer is just not something that appeals to you. You may be too busy running your business to become a copywriter. Or maybe you don't enjoy writing, or you don't think it's something you want to spend the time to learn.

That's no problem. There are professional copywriters who will be happy to write your piece for you. A simple search online and you'll find dozens to pick from.

One excellent place to start your search online is on the Direct Marketing Association of America (DMA) website at the-dma.org. It has an extensive list of vendors, including copywriters.

When you're considering hiring a copywriter, determine whether that person is familiar with your product and audience, and ask for samples of his or her work. Many copywriters specialize in a certain niche, like educational products, financial programs, or health supplements. Try to find someone who knows your field.

Of course, another important aspect of your sales piece is how it looks. An attractive layout is the first thing that will catch your reader's eye.

A well laid-out piece will guide the reader through the copy with color, headlines, and subheads. And it will be inviting: attractive and easy to read.

It should be easy for you to find a graphic designer who can design your piece for you. Again, you can search online to find a designer, perhaps starting on the DMA site.

Once you have your sales piece created, it's time to plan your entire mail package. That's what we'll look at next.

Sales Piece
Format and Design

*I*T WOULD BE GREAT IF YOU COULD PERSONALLY VISIT EACH AND EVERY prospect for your product or service. You could share your enthusiasm about the quality of your merchandise and your customer service team. You could explain the reasons why what you offer can have a positive impact on your buyer's life. You could go into detail about why you are so much better than any of your competitors.

Of course it's impossible for you to go out and meet everyone who could potentially become your customer. But in a way, that's what your sales piece does for you. It enters your prospect's home, sits at the kitchen table, and carries on a kind of "conversation" with him or her.

Your sales piece explains a problem your prospects have, offers a solution, anticipates and answers questions, and tells them exactly what steps they should take next so that you can make their lives better.

But there is one important difference between a live salesperson and a sales piece. If you were knocking on their door, they couldn't ignore you. But a sales piece could easily get pushed aside and never get read. It is an art to develop a sales piece that gets noticed.

You want your prospects to come home after a long day, stop at the mailbox to see what's waiting for them there, and have the first thing they notice be your sales piece. Maybe it's a bulky envelope with a big headline. Maybe it looks like an elegant invitation. Whatever its format, it catches your prospect's attention immediately.

And that's what we want to look at now. It's time to consider a very important element in the profitability of your direct-mail campaign: the physical package that you will be sending to your prospects.

It needs to be attractive enough to stand out in the pile of daily mail most people receive. In addition, it has to be the right format for your audience. Some formats just work better with some types of prospects (a matter of testing, which we'll look at in a later chapter).

And then there are issues concerning the actual printing of your package. How can you be sure that your print shop will produce what you want?

You don't have to become a printing expert. But there are some things you need to know so that you can be confident that you'll end up with a package to mail that will be worthy of what you have to sell.

Formats and Designs

There are many different formats and designs to choose from when planning a direct-mail campaign. Finding the right format for your offer, niche, and budget is critical to the success of your campaign.

For example, if you are trying to make a direct sell for a product or service, you may need more than a postcard to get the prospects to respond. On the other hand, if you are just trying to get people into your store for a free promotion, you most likely don't need a 10-page sales letter. A postcard that people can read at a glance may be your best option.

Below is a listing of some of the most popular mail formats.

The Letter Package

The most common format is a basic letter package. The components within it can vary, but in general, the package would consist of a letter, an order card or form, a brochure, and the outer envelope. Sometimes, there's a lift note included. A lift note is usually a little note (perhaps 6 x 9 inches) that looks very personal—and may even be made to look as though it has been written out by hand on stationery.

There are a number of different types of letter packages based on the size of the envelope used. The most common sizes are the #10 letter package, which uses a standard business-size envelope; a 6- x 9-inch letter package, which stands out a little bit more in the mail; or a large envelope letter package sized at 9 x 12 inches—which really stands out in the mail.

You can mail just about any size envelope you want. You can create a specific size just for your mailing, realizing, of course, that using a nonstandard size will cost a lot more to print.

The envelope can be plain white or it can be cream or black or blue or even a shiny silver or purple; you can make it any color you want. The more color and style you add to the envelope, the more it will cost to produce, but the more it will stand out in the mail. A shiny purple envelope will get looked at before a plain white envelope.

Some marketers do interesting things with envelopes by making them "official" looking. They may put words on them like "Verified Mail" and "Confirmation Number." Or they may create a sense of urgency with words like "Express Letter Service," "Rush," and "High Priority Contents." These are all ways to make sure your package gets noticed and moved to the top of the pile. On the other hand, sometimes a plain envelope does best, and there's only one way to know for sure: test different formats to see which brings the best response.

The Self-Mailer

Another format that's commonly used in direct mail is what is called a self-mailer. This is a piece of mail that is not enclosed in an envelope. It is mailed just like a magazine. There are many types of self-mailers; here are three of my favorites.

SLIM JIM

Ranges in size from 6 x 10 to $6^1/8$ x $11^1/2$ inches. The J. Peterman catalog is famous for its use of the slim jim format. There's a quality of elegance to this size and shape.

MAGALOG

Very commonly used. The size is around 8 x 11 inches. I'm sure you have seen these in your mailbox. It's floppy, it's full of color, and it's made to look like an actual magazine—but it's not. It's actually a sales letter. This is very commonly used in health supplement and nutritional marketing.

DIGEST

This is my personal favorite. I've mailed over 100,000,000 of the digest sales piece. It looks like a little booklet, kind of like *Reader's Digest*. The size is usually around 6 x 9 inches. This kind of piece is very appealing to people. It feels good in the hand and looks like it would be fun to read.

Self-mailers are very versatile, and there are a variety of ways you can use them. Keep in mind, with this, and really just about any mail format, the kind of paper you select can help create a certain impression. The piece can be printed on thick paper or thin paper, white paper or colored paper, matte paper or glossy paper. And it can be offset printed or digitally printed. There are numerous options with self-mailers that you can discuss with your print shop.

The Postcard

Generally, the least expensive type of direct-mail format is a postcard or a double postcard. Postcards offer a huge range of sizes. The 4- x 6-inch postcard is the least expensive to print and mail, and it's the size most commonly produced. A 5- x 7-inch postcard is the second most commonly used of all the postcard sizes. I've also used a huge $10^{1}/_{2}$- x 14-inch postcard.

Just because a piece is in a postcard format doesn't mean the postage is always going to be the lowest postcard rate. As you increase the size of the postcard, you'll also increase the cost of your postage. Depending on the size, it could even be charged at the full first-class postage rate.

Postcards are just like self-mailers but with a lot less sales copy. You get the benefit of the prospect seeing your sales copy right away instead of having to open an envelope. Your prospect can read the headline and see what the offer is at a glance.

CD Mailers

The CD mailer is another favorite of mine. I've mailed well over a million CDs to prospects. This format is really a cross between a standard mail piece and dimensional mail, which we'll discuss below. It mails flat, but when it's received you can feel something lumpy inside. That's what helps get this mail package opened. CD mailers are most commonly mailed in a 6- x 9-inch envelope. The mailer should include a short letter or lift note and be personalized. The CD should have sales copy on it with a phone number or web address. Many people end up throwing away the letter and envelope and holding on to the CD. Or prospects may listen to the CD in their car and decide to respond to the message on the spot. You need to make it easy for them to respond, so always include contact information on the CD.

The CD mailer can deliver a powerful message. Not only do you get to connect with prospects through a letter, they also get to hear your voice and listen to your enthusiasm about whatever you are offering. Your CD could also include testimonials from satisfied customers. Testimonials will encourage the prospects to respond.

The sales letter that goes with the CD mailer should focus on getting people to listen to the CD. That's the best way to get prospects to respond to your offer. The letter is only to pique their curiosity; you don't want to present the offer in the letter. If you do, the prospect will have no reason to listen to the CD and will completely miss the most powerful sales tool in the package. The whole idea is to get prospects to hear you deliver your message. It's almost like having an infomercial delivered right to their doorstep.

I've seen the CD mailer work in large-scale mailings, where we've mailed out hundreds of thousands, and I've also seen them work very well for clients with a very small mailing of only 200 pieces. The format is unique, it's compelling, it stands out in the mail, and it delivers a great response.

Dimensional Mail

If you want to mail something that is really going to stand out in the mailbox, then dimensional mail is your best option. I use dimensional mail to get people's attention in hard-to-reach niches, such as medical professionals or business executives who have gatekeepers who screen their mail.

Dimensional mail is not just a flat piece of mail that arrives in a mailbox. It has something totally unique about it, usually something lumpy—something that relates to your business or your offer or that has some clever tie-in to your sales copy. For example, if you are using an envelope, maybe you could put a chopstick or Jelly Bellies inside. Or if it's a package, like a foam mailer, it can contain a bottle with a message inside.

Dimensional mail has a much higher opening rate than traditional direct mail, and it's easy to see why. A mail package with something lumpy inside will spark the curiosity of the person receiving it.

If you are going to use dimensional mail, keep in mind that the cost per piece is going to be much higher than doing traditional direct mail. It costs more money to package and will most likely put you in a higher weight class for postage. Plus the actual item that you include (chopstick, aspirin, bottle, etc.) will cost more to produce than standard printed material. In addition, your production cost to assemble the package will be higher. It takes time to insert something of an odd size into an envelope. But given the higher response rate, it could well be worth the extra expense.

Dimensional mail has many great advantages, and there are thousands of different items you can use to capture your prospects' attention. There are unlimited dimensional mail packages to choose from, so you just have to find the right one for your niche.

Dimensional mail can be used very successfully by small businesses targeting a small customer file. If you're looking for a high response from 500 to 1,000 people and you can afford a higher mailing cost, then dimensional mail is definitely the way to go. It will get the customers' attention and get them to respond.

On the other hand, if you're trying to reach tens of thousands or perhaps millions of people, dimensional mail probably isn't the most effective way for you to reach out simply because of the huge mailing costs involved. The lower response on a larger untargeted list isn't likely to offset the extra cost of using dimensional mail.

If you would like to get a better feel for what these direct-mail formats look like, and perhaps get inspired for your own campaign, you can download some PDF samples at TheDirectMailSolution.com.

The Shock-and-Awe Package

This marketing method, first described by Dan S. Kennedy, is an elaborate package that you send to people who have specifically requested information from you about your products and services, and/ or have already placed an order with you. Regardless of how you got their attention initially—a direct-mail campaign, an ad in a magazine or newspaper, a radio spot, or even the internet—they have responded and come into your court.

The idea is to exceed their expectations, engage their interest, and build their loyalty—and perhaps even a sense of obligation to you—by sending them a package of materials and goodies that is unexpected and so impressive that it takes their breath away. That's why it's referred to as the "Shock and Awe" package.

The contents of your shock and awe package will vary with the nature of your business and your budget and on whether it's for lead generation or is part of a new-customer welcome package. Are you trying to sell the person something? You will need sales material. Is it a new customer package? You might need to provide orientation materials of some kind.

Another consideration is the image you want to convey. Do you want to appear serious and focused and therefore only want to include practical, necessary information and items? Or do you want to appear more friendly and playful? If so, you might broaden the range of possibilities to add some fun elements. Whatever you put in your package, it should be branded with your name and logo. You want the recipient to think of you every time he or she uses your mug, looks at your imprinted calendar, or reads through the materials you sent.

These packages should include as many items, and as wide a variety of items, as possible. The idea is to make going through the package seem like opening a present. It's better to break up the material into lots of different smaller pieces (booklets, CDs, tables, checklists). You want it to be exciting to go through and look like there's a lot going on there.

These packages can be expensive to put together. But they also can be one of the best ways to spend your marketing dollar. What makes this method work so well is that you're giving your expensive packages to a very self-selected group of people who are already interested in you. You have to do the math on your own situation to see how elaborate

How a Simple Design and Copy Change Can Have a Significant Impact on Your Direct-Mail Campaign

I once sent out a mailing for a client who wanted to test two different envelope packages. Both packages had precisely the same 16-page sales letter inside, the same order form, and the same reply device. The only difference was the outside of the envelope. One envelope had a really strong headline to grab the prospect's attention. The other envelope was completely plain and just listed my client's name, rather than the company's name.

By not putting any copy on the outer envelope and not putting the company name in the return address, it made the sales piece look rather obscure. You couldn't tell who the letter envelope was from, what was inside, or why it was being sent to you.

Which format do you think got the better response?

I've tested this concept a number of items. It's surprising to most people that every time I've tested it, the envelope with no headline or copy always pulls a much higher response rate. Most people would guess the opposite.

It should be noted that this test was based on mailing to cold-prospect lists. If you are mailing to your house file or a list of customers who know who you are, then I would recommend using an envelope with sales copy on it.

But why would a plain envelope work better to cold prospects?

Simple Design and Copy Change, continued

If prospects see a headline or a company name on the envelope, they know immediately that some kind of sales information is enclosed, and they make the decision right then and there whether they want to read it.

However, if there's a chance the letter might be from someone personal—a friend, a relative, or someone else, perhaps some mysterious stranger—then it's going to get opened. Once it gets opened and they take a look at it, they're going to realize, oh, this is some kind of sales material. At that point they may or may not read it, but the plain design got the envelope opened!

We have to get past that first barrier; we have to get our prospects to open the envelope. So, making the envelope plain—which keeps them from knowing exactly what it is— gives us a chance to get them to open it to see what's inside. That increases the chances they will read the sales copy—and possibly respond by ordering.

a package is worthwhile for you. Of course, you can completely tailor your shock and awe package to fit your business and budget. As always, only testing will determine if your shock and awe package brings a level of response that justifies the cost.

Issues of Design

Designing a direct-mail sales piece is not like designing an ad for magazines. It's not like a miniature version of a flashy website.

Direct-mail design is much different from what you see in mainstream advertising. For most businesses—not all businesses, but for most—you actually want the piece to be fairly plain, simple, easy to read, and not complicated with a lot of different graphics and fancy fonts.

The purpose of a direct-mail sales piece is to get people to read it and respond. Some companies that do direct mail try to "brand" their company by using beautiful art and large company logos and very little sales copy. This usually gets them little or no response, and it's really a waste of time and money. If you're serious about doing direct mail to get a response—to get customers to your store or drive them to your website—you need to have a very simple, clean, and easy-to-read sales piece design.

An important part of the design is the typeface or font that is used and how big it is—its point size. When I look at the font being used in a piece, I want to make sure it's large enough for the average customer to read, preferably a 12-point font, and at least a minimum of 10-point. You don't want to use a tiny 8-point font that's so hard to read, people will just throw the piece away. And you don't want to use something super fancy that almost looks like cursive writing or a decorative element. You want to use a simple, easy-to-read, serif-type font for the main body copy. Sometimes a designer will use a clean sans serif font for headlines. In Figure 3–1, you'll see examples of both serif and sans serif fonts.

Use graphics or photos to help support a key point in the copy, but don't overdo it. If you make your sales piece too graphic-oriented, people may totally miss the point of why you're contacting them. You want to be very clear with a direct-mail piece. The key to a good sales letter is to get people to respond, and it's strong sales copy that will do the job, not a design element or a fancy photo. You don't want your graphics to distract from the main point, which is to make a strong argument for buying your product or service. (You'll find the basic rules of writing effective sales copy in Chapter 2.)

FIGURE 3-1 Font Samples

Font Samples	
Now is the time for all good men	Times – Serif font. Good for body copy
Now is the time for all good men	Gill Sans bold – Sans serif font. Good for headlines
Now is the time for all good men	Times –7 pt. type size. Too small. Hard to read.
Now is the time for all good men	Courier–Serif font. Good for "typewriter" look. Easy to read.
Now is the time for all good men	Comic Sans-Sans serif font. Fun, casual look. Easy to read.
Now is the time for all good men	Lucida Calligraphy. A nice font for a fancy look that's still legible.
Now is the time for all good men	Bickham script. Too fancy. Hard to read.
Now is the time for all good men	Bauhaus. Could work for short headlines. It is a little hard to read.
Now is the time for all good men	Sample "handwriting font." Good for the look of a quick note. But not good for extended copy.
NOW IS THE TIME FOR ALL GOOD MEN	Stencil. Good for the right purpose, but not for extended copy.
Now is the time for all good men	Cracked. Another novelty font, good for limited use but not for extended copy. If you use, make it a large font size (14pt or larger).

Printing Your Mail Package

One of your priorities is selecting the right vendor for the job. Your mailing can be a success only if your vendors do their jobs correctly. It is critical to have excellent vendors who do superior work. These include list brokers, mail processors, and, of course, printers.

One of my clients used a printer who was a "family friend." I tried to tell him that the printer was providing poor quality and didn't pay attention to detail, but my client didn't listen. Eventually the printer made a huge mistake and put the wrong order form in with the sales piece. This "small" mistake went out to over 50,000 people. I ended up firing this client and refusing to work with him again.

I suggest that you keep vendor relationships on a business level. Over the years I've ordered thousands of mailing lists, printed millions of sales pieces, and processed too many jobs to count. Early in my career, I served as a purchasing manager and ordered hundreds of thousands of books, manuals, CDs, and DVDs. It's been my experience that vendors are always willing to become your buddy. They want to constantly talk with you on the phone and develop a friendship, which is very nice. But it can compromise your decision-making process in finding the best rate for your business, your clients, or whomever you're working with.

Let's say you're planning a direct-mail campaign and you need to give the job to a printer. One vendor is your friend, and he has a slightly higher price but provides lower quality of work. Meanwhile, there's another vendor out there who's a little better at a lower price. Which one will you select? You can see where at times, you'd lean toward giving your friend the business, but you'd end up paying more and risking a lower quality of printing.

Some people will disagree with me on this, but when it comes to my business, I want the best deal, and I want the job done right—the first time! That's why I keep vendor relationships on a professional level. The relationship is absolutely respectful, but we are not crossing the line and developing a friendship where we're hanging out, going to dinner, playing golf, etc. I don't want to compromise my judgment when it comes time to make the right decision for printing, duplicating, or any other services. So be careful with your vendor relationships and try to keep them business-related. It will benefit you in the long run, letting you establish great business relationships with a variety of vendors, rather than being stuck using just one vendor you're tightly connected with.

Deciding who will print your sales material can be complex. Weigh all these areas before making a final choice.

- $ *Color work.* Color adds an added dimension to most promotional pieces, but if it's not done right, it can cheapen the look of your piece. Make sure your printer can match the colors you want and does a nice, clean job.
- $ *Availability of stock.* Is your printer able to provide a wide variety of quality papers in different weights, textures, and colors? You'd be surprised at how the paper you use can affect the overall impression you present.
- $ *Proofs.* It could be problem if your printer is unwilling to let you see proof copies before printing a full job. While you don't want to be making editorial changes from proofs, you want to make sure the piece looks good and has the right codes, that the pages are in the right order, there are no smudges on the plates, and so on.
- $ *Quality of finishing work (folding, cutting, collating, etc.).* A job can be beautifully printed, but if it's cut at an angle, the corners aren't straight, or the folding is sloppy, it can ruin the job.
- $ *Responsiveness.* Things change quickly in business. You may have a last-minute brainstorm that requires a change in the piece you're printing. Or you may realize you put the wrong phone number on the piece. You want to know you can call and talk to a real person who will make the changes you want. This is no time to have to deal with a stream of voice-mail prompts or have to leave a message for someone you don't know and hope they get it and respond before the job goes to press. Contact your prospective vendor two or three times to see if he is available, and if not, how quickly he'll get back to you.
- $ *His niche market.* A printer who specializes in four-color printing that's high quality with low volume wouldn't be a good fit for

a two-color job that requires hundreds of thousands of pieces. Sure, he probably could do the job, but he wouldn't be as efficient at it as a printer who specializes in high volume work. It would be like taking your Ford truck to a Volkswagen mechanic. The VW mechanic could probably fix your truck, but he would not be as efficient as someone who fixes Ford trucks every day.

- *Pricing.* I always like to get a quote from three different vendors so I know that I'm getting a reasonable price. If one price is much lower than the others, be careful and double-check everything to make sure the vendor isn't missing any important details. Ask lots of questions so you can be certain there are no hidden costs. Compare vendors in the same niche. If you want to print 5,000 postcards, don't compare quotes from a vendor who specializes in printing postcards with a printer specializing in printing magazines.
- *Attention to detail.* When you ask for a quote, you have to give specifics about what is involved in the job. If the vendor misses or "forgets" to quote on one of the job's details, you may want to pass on using them. There are plenty of vendors to choose from. Make sure to use one that pays extra attention to detail.
- *Experience.* If your vendor has been in his niche business for many years, he will be more likely to catch any possible errors early on. He will also provide insight into how to run your job more efficiently. It's worth paying a little more for an expert. He will end up saving you money in the long run.

Finally, when considering whether to try a new printer, get samples of his work. Try to get samples of jobs similar to your own.

Get References

The price of the job is important but so are references. Make it a point to ask for references and actually call them. Many companies ask for references, but then never make the calls. If they had, they may have learned something that could have prevented a disaster. Ask a printer's reference questions like these:

- $ Was the quality what you were looking for?
- $ Did the job get done on time?
- $ How did the price compare to that of other printers?
- $ Were there extra, unexpected costs? Any hidden costs?

Visit the Printing Facility

If possible, you'll want to visit the printer and walk through the facility while it's operating. I've always found that a good printer keeps the floors clean and the warehouse organized.

I once visited the printing facility that prints the West Coast edition of the *New York Times*. It was a massive facility, but it was extremely dirty. It was perfect for printing newsprint and high-volume projects, but it would fail miserably if it tried to print a four-color, high-quality catalog or invitation. Visiting the printing operation will give you a much better idea about the printer's strengths and weaknesses and whether this facility is the one for you.

Once you find a great printer, find one or two more. You never want to be locked into using just one. I've had numerous mailings where the printer's schedule was too full to take my job and get it done when needed. Because I always have more than one printer, I'm able to move my job somewhere else without worrying about whether the job will be done right or on time.

Plus, having more than one great printer will keep them all competing for your business—giving you excellent pricing, quality, and customer service.

What About Those Discount Online Printers?

Many businesses are budget conscious these days—and properly so. But there's a great old expression: "penny-wise and pound foolish." In other words, trying to save a few cents by using a cheaper printer could end up costing you a lot more in printing jobs that look bad and don't get the response you want or, even worse, that you can't use at all.

I personally prefer a full-service printer with whom I have an ongoing relationship for higher-quality jobs that are more complex. I like being able to talk to the person who is doing the printing. I like to see paper samples so I know I'm getting the product I want. I like being able to get proof copies, especially for color jobs, before printing out 10,000 pieces. And I like being able to call with last-minute changes or corrections and know that someone will be there who knows the job and will be able to make sure the change is made before the job is printed.

Plus, when you have that kind of relationship with your printer, you have another set of eyes watching the job for you. The printer may notice a problem in how the art is laid out or that a color doesn't seem quite right. Instead of having the attitude "Well, the customer signed off on it so I'm not going to bother to check any further," your full-service printer is more likely to think, "I don't believe Craig will be happy if this job comes back looking like that. And even though it would be his responsibility, and I'd still get paid, I want to make sure he gets the job he wants. I'd better give him a call."

This isn't to say that discount online printers don't have their place. Discount printers can be good for small, simple jobs, like postcards that don't have any personalization. You can save a little money and still get an adequate-looking product. But for anything more complex, I like to use someone I know and trust.

Next we'll look at a surprising—but highly effective use of a direct-mail campaign.

How to Use Direct Mail to Drive Traffic to Your Website—and Then Back to Your Store!

YOU'VE PROBABLY HEARD THE FAMOUS QUIP BY MARK TWAIN: "THE reports of my death have been greatly exaggerated."

We might say the same thing about direct mail.

The reports of the death of direct mail are largely due to the digital age we're living in and the perceived changes it's brought to the way we communicate with each other. With the rise of the internet, many people think the days of snail mail are over. After all, shouldn't we advance with the times? Isn't it easier to just set up a pay-per-click (PPC) campaign or shoot off an email? And isn't it more effective?

I'll let you to determine what's easier for you. But one thing I can tell you from what I've seen is that those online methods aren't all that effective. In fact, if you want to build your online business, research shows that one of the best ways to do it is to use direct mail to drive prospects to your site. It's the combination of direct mail with an online presence that packs such a powerful marketing punch.

That's probably why many of the world's largest companies with a major internet presence regularly use direct mail to promote themselves. Even Google, probably one of the iconic internet businesses, sends out direct-mail campaigns. It uses a sales piece sent by physical mail to offer prospects $100 worth of free PPC advertising. By mailing these offers directly to people's homes or offices, it is able to reach a different audience than it does with its online efforts.

And this kind of promotion works. As we saw earlier in this book, people put greater trust in information they receive by mail. And they are more likely to read physical mail, unlike so much of email that gets deleted without being looked at. Direct mail must work because the great marketing minds at Google wouldn't use it if it weren't profitable.

Another huge online marketer is Serena & Lily. It doesn't even have any physical stores. All of its business is online only. While it does some online marketing, it reports that "65 to 70 percent of the company's total sales can be traced to print catalog marketing." Let me point out two critical details about this interesting quote:

1. It is entirely an online store, yet the majority of its sales come from a physical, direct-mail catalog.
2. It has traced its sales back to its print catalog. This means it is doing a great job of tracking its mail campaigns. It would not know the success of its direct mail if it hadn't put the effort into tracking. Savvy direct marketers track all the details in their mail campaigns so they know what is working and what is not! And that's what they stick with. We'll be looking at how to track your mail campaigns in Chapter 9.

The USPS Study

In a recent study, the United States Postal Service surveyed 5,000 visitors after they left 135 retail websites to determine how they came to the site and how much they spent on merchandise while there. The results were quite definitive in favor of direct mail. In fact, when it comes to online sales, the USPS invites people to think of direct mail as "power food for your website." Its findings show that direct mail can provide a solid boost to online traffic and sales. And it builds business by attracting new prospects who may never have visited a site otherwise.

According to the study's findings, prospects who received a catalog in the mail purchased 28 percent more items and spent 28 percent more money than those who did not receive one. Revenue from customers driven to sites by receiving a catalog was more than two times greater than the revenue from people who had received only online communications.

Here were some other interesting findings.

- More than 60 percent of people who received a catalog were influenced by the catalog to visit the website. The influence proved to be greatest on first-time shoppers.
- Catalogs were found to greatly discourage comparison shopping—by more than 10 percent. That means that site visitors came to the site and stayed on track—possibly because they had gone through the catalog and knew what they wanted to buy. They were less likely than random site visitors to go off searching other sites to find better prices or other selections.
- Catalog recipients were significantly more likely to shop for holiday gifts at the website than noncatalog recipients.
- Recency matters; 17 percent of people who received a catalog in the previous month purchased at least one item, while of those who received a catalog more than a month ago only 11 percent purchased an item.
- Compared to people who had not received a catalog, buyers who did receive a catalog reported that they were significantly
    - more satisfied with the company's website,

· more satisfied with their experience of the company, and
· more likely to recommend the website and the company to
  others.

This study shows all the advantages of using direct mail to build web traffic.

$ It lets you reach a wider range of prospects.

$ It builds confidence in you as a retailer.

$ It puts something in the prospects' possession that is a constant reminder of your site. Prospects can hold the sales piece in their hands and take it with them to read as they sit in their living room, on the back porch, or wherever they like to read.

$ The piece sits on the coffee table or kitchen counter where they see it again and again, unlike an email that is quickly deleted or an online ad that disappears a soon as the next URL is clicked.

I think it's important to make this last point. Although this study focused on catalog mailings, it also found similar results for other types of direct mailings, such as postcards. I mention this here because I don't want you to think that you need to produce a catalog to take advantage of the direct-mail boost in online traffic. I will show you how to take advantage of this medium using very simple mail pieces. In fact, the simpler, the better.

How My Own Clients Use Direct Mail to Bank Internet Profits

I know that the findings of the USPS study were right on point. That's because I've seen similar results with my own clients. In fact, let me tell you about the experience of one of them, a large publisher. It wanted to do its own test to determine the value of customers who came to the company in various ways. The idea was to determine the best use of its advertising dollar so it could design its future marketing plan.

For this study it looked at the lifetime value of customers who had bought its product—how much these customers spent with the company over an extended period of time. Its subjects included

$ 50,000 buyers who had come to it through a direct-mail piece,

$ 50,000 buyers who had come to it through a TV infomercial, and

$ 50,000 buyers who had come to it through an email campaign.

All the buyers had paid the same price for the product and had bought within a specific time frame. Now 18 months later, their lifetime value was compared, and this is what my client found: The buyers who came through a direct-mail piece had a lifetime value that was three to four times greater than that of the buyers who came through the internet campaign and two times greater than those who came through the TV campaign. The direct-mail buyers were the highest quality leads and spent 300 percent to 400 percent more money. Even if it may have cost more to generate these prospects, their significantly higher lifetime value more than justified the extra effort and expense.

And now let me share with you the experience of another client who sent out a mailing of almost 45,000 pieces to drive people to its website. The goal was to get people to "opt in" by providing an email address and other information upon visiting the site.

The campaign resulted in 5,345 prospects opting in, which was an excellent response rate of 11.94 percent. Of those, 231 prospects placed orders, meaning there was a 4.32 percent conversion from prospects into buyers. But that's not the end of it. The company now had 5,000 highly qualified leads that they could continue contacting with offers and promotions. So not only did they receive over 200 actual orders, but they also now had access to a highly promising storehouse of names on which to grow future business.

In my experience just about any business with a website can build response by incorporating a direct-mail component into its marketing plan. To show you how it works, in the next section we'll look at how you would use direct marketing if you already have a website set up for internet marketing. We'll then look at what you would have to do if your website is not yet set up for any kind of marketing. Finally, I'll show you how even a brick-and-mortar retailer can use direct mail to build an email list to be used for ongoing email promotions.

How It Works If You Already Have a Website Designed with a Sales Funnel

Let's assume that you already have an active online presence, and you have been using online means to promote your site. You may be driving customers to your site with a pay-per-click campaign: You place a banner ad on other internet sites, and you pay a fee each time someone clicks your ad and is taken to your site. Or you may reach out to prospects by running email campaigns. Or you may have affiliate promotions with other marketers where they promote your site to their buyer or member lists. Or you may use all three methods.

In any case, you are doing something to drive traffic to your site, and it's working well. And as a savvy marketer, you have your site all set up to meet these prospects when they arrive. You probably have some kind of landing page that prospects arrive at when they click your link or ad. It has clear steps the prospect should follow to opt in.

The opt-in section is where prospects provide at least their name and email address. You may also be able to get their physical addresses you can use to help you market to them in the future. By giving you this information, prospects are giving you both permission to contact them again and the means to do so. Because they have come to you and are willing to provide you with this information, they are hot prospects and very valuable to you.

Once your prospect has opted in and has been moved along to a sales page, hopefully you are able to turn the prospect into a customer.

Perhaps this is all working OK, but you wish you could get even more new prospects to visit your site. You've been hearing that direct mail may be one way to attract a whole new audience, but you know very little about direct mail. You're concerned that it might be a lot to take on. However, embarking on a direct-mail campaign would actually be extremely easy for you. You're already perfectly set up for it. You have your landing page, and people are coming to it via your online marketing. You just have to set up a stream of prospects that comes to you through direct mail, and all that you need to do is write a direct-mail piece with a clear call to action that drives people online.

So let's talk about this sales piece that has to be created. Fortunately, you don't need a long, complicated piece. In fact, that's just what you don't want. Really, you could just use a postcard—small, large, or even oversized—but still just a postcard. Or, if you feel more copy is needed to do the job, I'd recommend going no larger than a four-page self-mailer. And remember, as a self-mailer, one page would be allocated for some teaser copy and space for the address, the return address, and postage. So, it's really just three pages of copy—not counting any photos or illustrations that may fill up some space.

Whichever format you use, you want compelling, intriguing copy with the primary aim of getting people to go to your website. You don't necessarily want to sell the product or give all the details of the offer. If you give too much information at this point, prospects may decide they're not interested and not visit the site. But the site is where you do your main selling, so you want to keep them curious and excited and eager to find out more.

Once prospects arrive online, I advise my clients to always ask them to opt in before moving on to the next stage. You at least want to capture their email address. Then, if possible, you want their full name and their mailing address. Prospects may not be willing to give that right away, so get what you can. Now you can present them with your sales page.

Your sales page can take several forms. One popular method is a video sales letter where prospects are shown a video of someone presenting the product or service and making the offer. Another method is a text letter that appears like a PowerPoint presentation with narration, so it's a cross between a letter and a video. Or you could show them a previously recorded webinar. Or just use a simple text sales letter.

The point of the sales page is to convince prospects to move along to the next stage so that they will ultimately provide you with the information you want, such as their mailing address. And, of course, it would be great if you could get them to take you up on your offer to buy something.

At several points in the process you can try to get the information you want. For example, you may thank them for opting in and tell them if they provide their physical address you will send them coupons to your store. Or you'll send them a free report with valuable information. This is your chance to be creative about capturing prospects' information now that you've gotten them to visit you online. For examples, visit www.TheDirectMailSolution.com.

Can you see what you've done here? You were able to capture a prospect from a direct-mail list, and you got the person to visit your website and give you the information you need to contact him or her again. You know that this is an excellent prospect who is interested in you. And significantly, this is a person who may never have found you had you not reached out to find him yourself.

This is perfect for a business that already has an online sales funnel. You don't have to develop a whole new system to make sales. You can tap into the online funnel that's already working for you. You're just adding a new way to drive prospects to the sales structure that's already there.

But if you don't have marketing capability on your website, you have to go an additional step.

What to Do If Your Website Isn't a Sales Funnel

You may already have a great website with a nice home page and other informational or product pages. But if that's all you have, it may not be ready yet for use as part of a sales funnel.

When new prospects come to your site from your direct-mail piece, you probably don't want them to come directly to your home page. First, there's too much for prospects to see. They may be confused about what to do first. Or they may start clicking links, go off reading other pages, and then wander away.

You want to have much more control of your prospects' attention, and specifically you want to help ensure they are clearly guided to the opt-in area first. That means you want a special page that prospects are immediately linked to from the URL in the sales piece. This is your carefully designed landing page, most likely with some kind of opt-in area built in.

Once prospects opt in, you must decide where they go next. Is it to a video? A video letter? Just plain text? You want to carefully guide them along.

A good web designer should be able to create these pages. And if you use a writer to create a sales piece, that same writer should be able to supply the copy for your site, largely based on the sales piece. Or, based on what you've learned in this book, you could write the copy on your own.

How a Brick-and-Mortar Retailer Can Use a Direct-Mail Postcard to Build an Email List of Great Prospects

We've been looking at how to use direct mail to drive traffic to a website and build an email list or make online sales. But you can take it a step further to then drive that traffic right back into your physical store. I've generated tens of thousands of online prospects for my clients by sending postcards by direct mail. For many of them the idea was to eventually get those prospects into a store.

You could start by simply sending out a direct-mail postcard that directs customers to your website. Once they get to your website, you can have them opt in to receive a free gift or a special coupon.

For example, let's say that you're a furniture store and you're having a weekend sale. A great way to publicize the event is to send out a mail piece to everyone who has bought from you in the last three years. You should also mail everyone else on your list, such as people who have made inquiries or have contacted you in some way. At the same time, a smart marketer would maximize this campaign by not only driving current and past customers to the store but also reaching out to new prospects (who will hopefully become new customers). So perhaps you would mail to every address of people with incomes above a certain level within a five-mile radius.

You could send a direct-mail postcard to prospects that drives them to the website by saying: "Visit our website and print out our special coupon to receive an additional 10 percent off our already discounted weekend sale prices. Plus—get a FREE gift! $5 worth of Starbucks coffee!"

Prospects may look at that and say "Wow, I may not be interested in buying furniture right now, but I'm interested in that $5 worth of Starbucks coffee. So I'm going to visit the website." They go to the website, opt in, and get instructions for receiving their free coffee, which they have to claim at the store. You've just earned yourself the contact information for a new prospect who you can reach out to in the future.

Once these prospects are in the store, you have the opportunity to show them your fine furniture and special sale items and ask for their mailing address. The $5 worth of free coffee may sound like a big investment on your part, but these people are highly self-selected, and they are going to remember the gift and the good experience they had with you when they are ready to buy a piece of furniture. They are much more likely to come back and shop at your store because of the generous gift that you've given them.

This is just one of many ways to combine direct mail with the internet to build your mail and email lists and grow your business.

PURL Postcards

Another unique format that lets you combine the power of direct mail and the internet is the PURL postcard. PURL stands for Personal URL.

With this ingenious method, you take a normal URL (a regular website address), and you add the first and last name of the prospect to the URL to turn the URL into a Personal URL. For example: simpson direct.com can be made into a PURL for your prospect John Smith by adding his name: simpson-direct.com/john.smith. The name can also go in front of the URL: john.smith.simpson-direct.com. Thanks to creative programming, you don't have to develop separate pages for each prospect. The programming personalizes the page automatically.

Imagine getting a postcard in the mail with a URL printed on it that has your name in it. It would be almost irresistible, wouldn't it? The PURL postcard really captures prospects' attention and drives them to see a personal message on their "own" website. It sparks an interest and curiosity in prospects. After all, who wouldn't want to immediately see their own website?

Postcards and self-mailers both work great when using a PURL because the sales message can be made very personal by including prospects' names. The message on the mailer piece should include copy that says something like "John Smith, here's your personal website! Go to . . ."

When the prospect gets to the landing page, that's where the real sales piece is. The sales copy on the PURL website needs to be personalized and must have strong incentives to get customers to respond to whatever you are offering.

I've mailed over a million pieces for my clients using the PURL method, and it consistently generates great results.

Important Considerations for an Effective Direct-Mail/Internet Program

If you think that using direct mail in conjunction with the internet holds promise for your business, I encourage you to try it. Here are some points for you to keep in mind so that you can make the most of this powerful combination.

An Intriguing Message

The message in your direct-mail piece must capture prospects' attention and interest to such a degree that they will stop whatever it is they're doing and go online to visit your website. The mail piece itself won't be very long, so it has to pack a very powerful punch in minimal words. You need a headline that immediately arouses curiosity and promises some kind of benefit. Then you have to offer them an excellent reason to go to the site: They'll receive a coupon or a free report; they'll get to watch a video that will reveal some big secret that will make their life better. Motivate them to take the action you want.

The piece itself must look effortless, but writing it requires quite a bit of savvy. So put some work into coming up with a message that will move people to act.

A Clear Call to Action

Now that you've got your prospects' attention and they're ready to act, you have to provide them with a crystal clear call to action. What you want them to do is visit the site. Don't provide them with any alternative actions, and don't make them struggle to find your web address. People's attention spans are very short, and if they have to go hunting for the information they'll get annoyed or distracted. You want to keep them positive and moving in the right direction. Make the next step clear and easy to follow.

An Easy URL

Prospects going from a direct-mail piece to a website must type in the URL themselves. It's not like they can just click on a link. So you don't want a URL that's complicated, has an odd spelling, or that's too long. And you want it to be memorable so that if they are not near their computer when they read your sales piece, they'll be able to remember it when they need it.

An Incentive to Opt In

One of the most critical reasons for getting your prospects to the site is to capture their contact information. You want them to opt in. But they won't do it unless you provide them with a good reason to do it. Maybe for opting in they will receive a bonus of some kind, or they will receive some valuable information. It's important that you keep your opt-in web page copy short with clean directions on how to opt in. Some of the best opt-in pages I've used have only ten words on them. Keep it simple and keep the instructions clear.

A Compelling Sales Page

Once prospects have opted in and arrived at your sales page, you want them to be willing to read your letter, watch your video, or do whatever it is you've set up for them. So the page has to be attractive, interesting, and easy to read, with lists of benefits that can be seen at a glance.

A Coordinated Message

For a successful campaign you should have consistent branding and messaging. All the pieces should coordinate with one another and present one clear message and call to action. If your sales piece is whimsical, there should be a whimsical quality to your website. If your message is serious, all the pieces should be serious. The look of the direct-mail piece and the website should be similar. Of course, the offer and the call to action should be in agreement across all the different media.

With all the pieces in place and working together, you will increase the chances of a favorable response.

You May Be Closer Than You Think

If you already have an online presence, you've been using online marketing to get people to visit your website, and you are already set up with a landing page and opt-in program, you already have in place most of what you need to expand into a direct-mail component. You're just developing another way to drive traffic.

But remember, this is more than just another way to drive any traffic. Research shows that customers generated by direct mail, as opposed to online methods, are better customers who spend more money with you. That alone should make you want to look into this approach and take the necessary steps to incorporate it into your overall marketing program.

Also remember, the direct-mail sales piece doesn't have to be long. You can get started with just a postcard. That will keep the production costs down and make it easier to write.

Of course, if you don't already have a sales funnel as part of your website, you will need to add one, but even then we're just talking about a landing page and a sales page.

The internet is a significant medium playing a larger and larger role in our lives. But it will never replace direct mail as a way to communicate a memorable message that is noticed and that builds trust. When you are able to put the best aspects of the internet and direct mail together in one sales package, you multiply the effectiveness of your efforts.

This book also serves as an example of taking prospects offline and moving them online. You have the opportunity to read this book and then go online for more resources at www.TheDirectMailSolution.com.

At this point you should be filled with ideas about the sales piece you'll be sending out and what it will say. Which brings us to the next important question: To whom will you mail it? That's what we'll look at in Chapter 6.

The Message
and the Messenger

By Dan S. Kennedy

A s Craig has described, a direct-mail piece or package involves two big decisions and comprises two big pieces of work: the message, expressed in copy, graphics, and photos; and the messenger, which is the format. I'll give you my perspective on both.

Why Marketing Messages FAIL

If you are in the patio furniture business, you can't help yourself. You habitually think about patio furniture, and you assume others are interested in patio furniture, too. And you are wrong. This is where failed messages begin, by being product-driven rather than driven by human interest, real life, and emotion. People buy patio furniture to sit on only when their current patio furniture is falling apart or they've moved, have an empty patio, and didn't bring their old patio furniture with them. Not enough of these folks in a given area to support your patio furniture store, let alone everybody else selling the stuff. You must get people who do not NEED new patio furniture, who can sit in the patio furniture they've got, to (irrationally) WANT new patio furniture. A message about brand names, vast selection, low price, easy financing, and free delivery FAILS TO CREATE OR STIMULATE WANT—it only caters to NEED.

Hardly anybody spends $100,000 remodeling a kitchen because their current kitchen doesn't work. They do it out of WANT, not NEED.

Both these examples involve emotion—ego, status, outdoing the neighbors, pride of ownership. Family life and social life—having a better environment, making at home experiences more enjoyable, having the place family and friends want to congregate. Human interest—the story of the big Fourth of July party or the Thanksgiving gathering with feasts prepared by three generations in the amazing kitchen. If you want to see somebody who has mastered this, in the backyard deck and gazebo business, visit the website of one of our great GKIC Members, Matt Buchel: tropicallifestyle.com.au.

At the end of this chapter, in Figures 5–1 to 5–4, I've reprinted just a few pages from one booklet, part of a complete, multipiece direct-mail package sent to leads obtained online, at home shows, and from simpler lead-generation direct mail. This company is thriving, and selling at premium prices, because it has built such a comprehensive message.

Look at page 43 of this sales booklet: a human interest story about a couple getting married in their Tropical Lifestyle gazebo (Figure 5–4). The front cover positions the sales booklet as a "how to" consumer's guide and features a lifestyle photo of a happy family. Pages 15 and 24 focus on real-life reasons why specific types of customers might want a gazebo and deck (Figures 5–2 and 5–3). In total, this is a 52-page sales piece, loaded with really great sales copy, with a good balance between product information and the more persuasive copy to make people WANT a whole new, "tropical lifestyle" backyard. (All this is so successful, by the way, that a few years back, Matt won the coveted GKIC Marketer of the Year Award, and now has a package of all his marketing that he licenses to other contractors throughout the world, and a samples package that business owners in many different areas buy from him as well.)

Matt has mastered the making of messages about real life, customer emotions, and human interest.

Unless and until you understand this, and translate and apply it to your business, you will forever fail at assembling interesting, persuasive, and productive messages.

Direct mail fails, or at least disappoints for four reasons:

1. Poorly chosen list (Chapter 6 will cover this topic.)
2. An uninteresting, boring message that fails to motivate WANT
3. A message poorly matched with the list
4. A messenger that can't get the message across

Two of these four failure factors revolve around the message. This is why it's so critically important to craft a message worthy of investment.

There are a number of possible ways to get to a worthy message.

You can and should assemble "raw material." That may be past advertising that has worked, competitors' advertising, transcripts of recordings of you or your best salespeople talking on the phone or face to face with prospects, a focus group or interviews with customers, or testimonials from customers. Research what exceptionally successful operators of your type of business are doing in other parts of the country.

You ought not focus just on those in your own field—some of the best breakthrough ideas come from great marketing and great messages outside your field. To that end, you should tap into GKIC, a network and clearinghouse of great marketing, with a plethora of resources, meetings and conferences, and assistance, starting with a free test-drive opportunity. As a GKIC Member you're introduced to thousands of people in diverse businesses who are every bit as successful at this kind of marketing as Matt Buchel, who's work I've shown off here. Every month, in the No B.S. Marketing Letter, you see amazing examples of great marketing. Check in at www.dankennedy.com/ DirectMailSolution, Craig's GKIC affiliate site.

If you are going to write your sales copy yourself, you need three things: structure, inspiring samples to lead your thinking, and all of the raw material that I just mentioned. Giving you a crash course in direct-response copywriting here is way beyond this book's purpose, so instead, I'll recommend the best basic shortcut resources I can. One is mine, a book, *The Ultimate Sales Letter (4th Edition);* plus *The Architecture of Persuasion* by Michael Masterson; *How to Create Irresistible Offers* by Robert Bly; *and Great Leads: Six Easiest Ways to Start Any Sales* Message by Masterson and Forde. These books will give you structure for your copy. A skeleton to hang your flesh on.

In addition, many specific tools are available, like fill-in-the-blank headlines. *Million Dollar Mailings* by Denny Hatch and *The Greatest Sales Letters* by Hodgson are, in large part, giant inspiration files, with actual samples of extremely successful sales letters for various companies, products, and purposes. Last, there are "cheat sheets": two advertising thesauruses, *Words That Sell* and *More Words That Sell* by Richard Bayan. For many purposes, this will be enough. If you want to go further, both basic and advanced online and home-study courses on copywriting are available from two sources: GKIC, at www.DanKennedy.com/store, and from AWAI, American Writers and Artists, at www.AWAIonline.com.

If you are going to write by committee—involving your spouse, business partner, and key employees—do yourself a huge favor and get the book *Copy Logic: The New Science of Producing Breakthrough Copy (Without Criticism)* by Michael Masterson and Mike Palmer.

If you are going to hire a copywriter or copywriters, or a copywriting coach to critique your work, I suggest working through AWAIonline. com. It maintains directories of freelance copywriters and has an assignments board where you can post your needs and invite interested, appropriate copywriters to connect with you, provide samples of work, and even audition. If you are working with Craig Simpson, he can also direct you to appropriate copywriters. If you have a project of significant size and scope, I occasionally accept new copywriting clients myself—but I am at the top of the compensation range; we begin with a day of diagnostic and strategy consulting (as of this writing, my base fee for that day is $18,800); multimedia, multistep campaigns frequently involve fees from $50,000 to $150,000 and beyond, plus royalties, usually linked to resulting gross revenues.

If you are going to use outside copywriters, you still need to assemble good raw material for them, and it is still useful to be familiar with what they are doing and why they are doing it the way that they are—so I still recommend reading the above-listed books.

My final message recommendation is: Don't be Amish. Most businesspeople study only—only!—what their direct competitors and peers do. Everybody in a circle looking at each other. But great messages that work with direct mail tend to be *direct-response* messages, not traditional retail or service messages, so you need to observe and learn from direct-response marketers. Find relevant direct-marketing companies to watch and borrow ideas from. If you have a local butcher shop, pay attention to how Omaha Steaks sells steaks by mail order, direct mail, and online; don't pay attention to the other butcher shop across town. If you have an upscale menswear store, pay attention to the Charles Thywritt Company, to J. Peterman Co., and to other direct marketers in the category. If you are a dermatologist, look at how my client, Guthy-Renker, advertises its acne remedy, Proactiv®.

What Messenger to Entrust Your Message To

Message can govern formats, or formats can govern message. But one thing is definite: the format of your direct-mail piece or package should be carefully chosen, and its appearance should be congruent with its purpose—which often means less than aesthetic, artistically pure designs.

My friend and client, Jerry Jones, who has probably put more patients in dentists' chairs all over the world with his direct mail than anybody, living or dead, ever, often has trouble with his doctor-clients who want to use postcards with beautiful photos, logos, and very little copy, to look "professional." One of his consistently best-performing postcards is black typewriter-looking type on an ugly green 3- × 5-inch postcard. This is why we always test multiple "looks" and formats.

Ugly or pretty, plain or fancy, in an envelope or self-mailer, big or small—well, it all depends.

The most important thing to know is: The format's jobs are: 1) to get delivered, 2) to get opened or looked at, and 3) to facilitate the sales copy, the message creating interest and persuading the reader to take a clear next step. Don't add any other directives or responsibilities to that list—like pleasing you, your spouse, your staff, or your graphic artist, or making a brand statement, or winning awards, or being funny or clever. Any or all of those other things may or may not happen in the course of achieving the three essential goals, but none of these other things can direct the content or appearance or format of your direct-mail piece.

The second most important thing to do is to be reasonable. Do not underestimate the difficulty of achieving these three goals. A simple postcard with a coupon on it may be able to achieve these goals if it's going to homes with customers who know your business and regularly or seasonally buy what you sell—say, pizza or snow tires. But a simple postcard simply cannot be reasonably expected to survive a mailroom and a gatekeeper, to reach and interest a corporate CEO. What you are doing with direct mail is buying interest and response, and you have to understand that there is variable cost in getting different kinds of people's interest. The desire for unearned success is a rising plague on American society, adversely affecting us in a myriad of ways—including business owners' irrational disappointment with direct mail when formats wholly inappropriate for its task and its audience are used and too-cheap investments are made.

Incidentally, direct mail doesn't just mean mail. I've had and have many clients who use Federal Express, UPS, and the USPS' Priority Mail as delivery means for marketing messages. Nor does it just refer to printed matter. We send audio CDs, video DVDs, DVDs in players inside attaché cases, messages inscribed on or fastened to basketballs and coconuts and canoe paddles, and every other imaginable object. The value of the response tells us what we can spend, establishing what I call the Maximum Allowable Investment; we then engineer the most impactful campaign within that number. For a look at a wide variety of odd, unusual "object mail," visit www.3DMailResults.com.

On the other hand, sometimes simple is best. The late, great copywriter Gary Halbert was a staunch advocate of a simple, hand-addressed, live postage stamp-adorned envelope, with no business identity, no logos, and no teaser copy. Pure "sneak-up mail," appearing to be personal, from one individual to another.

Much of the time, my clients are doing multistep mailings, so there is the opportunity to use several different formats within the campaign.

Ultimately, you must think of your format as a real messenger. You are asking him to go to your prospect's home or office, knock on the door, and present himself—when he will either be invited in to tell his story or have the door rudely slammed in his face, denying him any opportunity. How will you dress and outfit and enable your messenger? My friend Sally Hogshead, author of the excellent book, *Fascinate*, has documented well that the average initial attention span to anything new is now down to the attention span of a goldfish: nine seconds. Keep that in mind.

FIGURE 5-1 The cover of Matt Buchel's 52-page Tropical
Lifestyle sales booklet.

FIGURE 5-2 Page 15 of Matt Buchel's Tropical Lifestyle sales booklet.

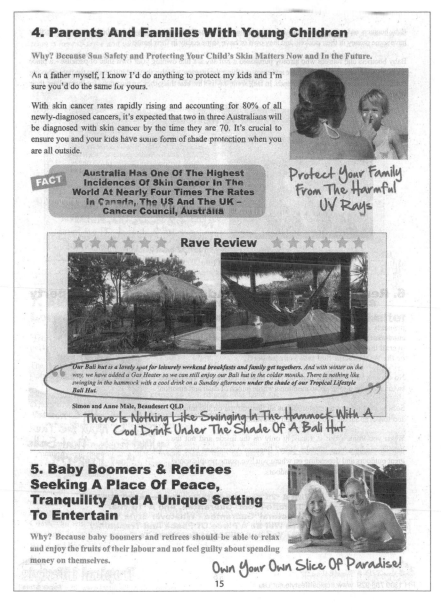

4. Parents And Families With Young Children

Why? Because Sun Safety and Protecting Your Child's Skin Matters Now and In the Future.

As a father myself, I know I'd do anything to protect my kids and I'm sure you'd do the same for yours.

With skin cancer rates rapidly rising and accounting for 80% of all newly-diagnosed cancers, it's expected that two in three Australians will be diagnosed with skin cancer by the time they are 70. It's crucial to ensure you and your kids have some form of shade protection when you are all outside.

FACT Australia Has One Of The Highest Incidences Of Skin Cancer In The World At Nearly Four Times The Rates In Canada, The US And The UK – Cancer Council, Australia

Protect Your Family From The Harmful UV Rays

★ ★ ★ ★ ★ ★ **Rave Review** ★ ★ ★ ★ ★ ★

Our Bali hut is a lovely spot for leisurely weekend breakfasts and family get togethers. And with winter on the way, we have added a Gas Heater so we can still enjoy our Bali hut in the colder months. There is nothing like swinging in the hammock with a cool drink on a Sunday afternoon under the shade of our Tropical Lifestyle Bali Hut.

Simon and Anne Male, Beaudesert QLD

There Is Nothing Like Swinging In The Hammock With A Cool Drink Under The Shade Of A Bali Hut

5. Baby Boomers & Retirees Seeking A Place Of Peace, Tranquility And A Unique Setting To Entertain

Why? Because baby boomers and retirees should be able to relax and enjoy the fruits of their labour and not feel guilty about spending money on themselves.

Own Your Own Slice Of Paradise!

15

FIGURE 5-3 Page 24 of Matt Buchel's 52-page Tropical Lifestyle sales booklet.

FIGURE 5-4 Page 43 of Matt Buchel's 52-page Tropical Lifestyle sales booklet.

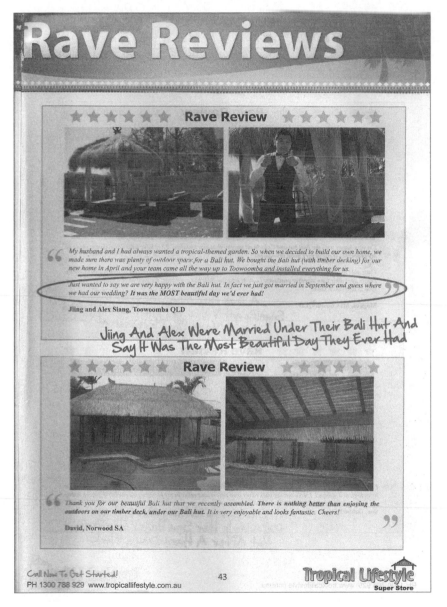

Mailing Lists
and Segmentation

WITH YOUR SALES LETTER IN HAND, IT'S TIME TO FIND YOUR BEST prospects to mail it to.

Suppose your product is a bicycle tire repair kit that enables cyclists to change a flat tire in half the time. Competitive cyclists everywhere will be eager to snatch up these new repair kits.

All you have to do is reach the right audience to tell them about your amazing product. You would like to reach a group that's primarily made up of bicycle enthusiasts who ride frequently and may even compete in races, or bike shop owners who change tires all day long.

You don't want to reach the guy who has a bike in the garage that he hasn't looked at in a year and not ridden in five years. You want to be as targeted as possible when selecting your direct-mailing list. In this example, you don't want to contact everyone who owns a bike . . . you want those who are actively riding their bikes and may need to change a tire quickly.

Here's another example. Let's say your product is a new kind of dog leash that makes walking and running with your dog easier. If you want to do a mailing to promote your new leash that gets the highest response rate, you wouldn't want to mail to everyone who owns a dog. Instead, you will want to mail dog owners who have bought items for their dogs through the mail in the past, more than one time, and recently. If your prospects have a proven buying history, then you have a better chance that they will purchase your product or service. If you mail to people who have dogs, but none of the other characteristics, you're most likely wasting your money because the list would be too broad and wouldn't target your best prospects.

In this chapter, we'll examine the different kinds of mailing lists that are available and the simple steps you can take to get your hands on one that's targeted to your audience. Use the right mailing list to send the right sales piece, and you will be on your way to a successful mail campaign.

Types of Mailing Lists

When planning a direct-mail campaign, you obviously need a group of prospects—along with their names and addresses—to offer your product or service to. These names, which represent people with similar characteristics, are rented or sold as a mailing list.

If you rent these names, you'll be able to mail to them at least once, and maybe up to three times, depending on the agreement you set up with the list owner. Sometimes, you are given the option to purchase the mail list. If you do, you'll have to pay more for the list, but you'll have unlimited usage.

One of the toughest and most critical tasks in putting together a successful direct-mail campaign is making sure you select the right lists to mail to. If you mail to a list of people who have no interest in your product, even the greatest copy will not work.

With thousands of mailing lists to choose from, you may not be sure where to start. And the stakes are high because selecting the wrong list will surely destroy your opportunity for success.

So let's start making sense out of all the possibilities.

There are many different types of lists available. Some direct-mail marketers break them up into many different categories. I like to break lists up into two main categories: house file and rented lists.

House File

Your house file, also referred to as your customer file, is the list of individuals you already have in your database. They are either your own current buyers, past buyers, or people who have made inquiries about your product. Talk about a targeted list! These people absolutely fit the definition of your target audience, and they will normally be the most responsive to your offer. Also, because these names are in your own database, you don't have to pay a rental fee to use them. So you want to make the best use possible of this great resource.

You should be keeping good records of everyone who ever buys anything from you or contacts you for any reason at all. Many companies fail in this area. I'll ask my clients how many people have purchased a specific product from them within the last three months. They'll have no clue and no way of accessing their database to find out. This is just poor business practice. You must have an organized, user-friendly, up-to-date database. And every time a prospect or customer contacts you, you should be sure to get her name and address and add it into your database.

If you do have a useable database, you should start organizing it right away. Depending on the number of products or services you offer, your house file should be segmented (that is, broken into significant categories) based on the relationship each person on the list has with your company.

There are many ways to segment your house file. How you do so will depend on the number of names you have in your house file and the kind of information you have on each person. Here's a simple segmentation option that has the house file split into three groups:

1. *Buyer File.* Purchased just one product/service
2. *Multibuyer File.* Purchased more than one product/service
3. *Inquiry File.* Interested prospects who have contacted you in some way—maybe by calling your company after seeing an ad, making an inquiry on a website, etc.

If you have the information on your list, you can break these groups down into smaller segments based on how the prospects were generated—internet, radio/TV, space ads, direct mail, etc. This could help you in planning future promotions:

Buyer File: Purchased just one product/service
   a. Internet-generated buyers
   b. Radio/TV-generated buyers
   c. Direct-mail–generated buyers
   d. Space ad/classified ad–generated buyers

Multibuyer File: Purchased more than one product/service
   a. Internet-generated multibuyers
   b. Radio/TV-generated multibuyers
   c. Direct-mail–generated multibuyers
   d. Space ad/classified ad–generated multibuyers

Inquiry File: Interested prospects who haven't made a purchase yet
   a. Internet-generated inquires
   b. Radio/tv-generated inquires
   c. Direct-mail–generated inquires
   d. Space ad/classified ad–generated inquires

But it doesn't stop there. There's additional important information you can glean from your list.

The best way to further segment your house file is to use an RFM Score.
RFM Scoring is:

R = Recency. Customers who purchased recently are more likely to
buy again vs. customers who have not purchased in a while.

F = Frequency. Customers who purchased frequently are more likely
to buy again vs. customers who have made just one or two purchases.

M = Monetary/Money. Customers who have spent the most money in
total on previous orders are more likely to buy again.

Customers can be ranked based on their R, F, and M characteristics
and assigned a "score" representing this rank. Assuming the behavior
being ranked using RFM has economic value, the higher the RFM score,
the more profitable the customer is to the business now and in the future.

High RFM customers are most likely to continue to purchase, and
they are most likely to respond to your marketing promotions.

Whenever I analyze a house file, I like to use an RFM score to
determine how strong the file is. In order to rank the customers for an
RFM score, you need to assign a score for each characteristic. Here's one
example of how you might score your customers:

Recency

All customers who have purchased in the last 6 months receive a
score of 3.

All customers who have purchased in the last 7 to 16 months
receive a score of 2.

All customers who have purchased in the last 17 to 24 months
receive a score of 1.

All customers who have not purchased for the past 25 months
receive a score of 0.

Frequency

All customers who have purchased 4 or more products receive a
score of 3.

All customers who have purchased 2 or 3 products receive a score of 2.

All customers who have purchased 1 product receive a score of 1.

Trial subscriptions/free offers receive a score of 0.

Monetary

Customers who have spent over $700 receive a score of 3.

Customers who have spent between $200 and $699 receive a score of 2.

Customers who have spent between $51 and $199 receive a score of 1.

Customers who have spent less than $50 receive a score of 0.

Of course, depending on your product, its cost, etc., you would adjust how you assign the scores.

Once all the scores have been assigned to each customer, add up each customer's score and then break the file into ranks:

Rank 1 = 9 Score

Rank 2 = 8 Score

Rank 3 = 7 Score

Rank 4 = 6 Score

Rank 5 = 5 Score

Rank 6 = 4 Score

Rank 7 = 3 Score

Rank 8 = 2 Score

Rank 9 = 1 Score

Rank 10 = 0 Score

The lowest rank (Rank 1) will be made up of customers who have the highest score and are your best customers. The higher the rank (8, 9, 10), the lower the score and the weaker the customer.

Again, this is just one example of how to segment a list. There are numerous ways to segment your house file, and it's up to you to choose what will be the most usable structure for your business model.

With your house file organized, you have a great start on developing your customer profile. After all, your best guide to future prospects is who your existing customers are now. So start making a list of characteristics of your best current buyers. Do they come from a certain geographic area? Do they tend toward male or female? How old are they? What is their income level? What are their interests and hobbies?

If you're not sure about these things, ask your customers. Put together a customer survey. Or just ask some questions when they call your customer service line or come into your store.

All this information is critical for properly using your next source of names to mail to: rented lists. With knowledge of your existing customers, you can effectively narrow down your mailing list selection. You want the mailing lists that you rent to be made up of people who look just like your existing customers. You want them to have the same buying habits, be the same gender and age, have a similar income and net worth, etc.

Rented Lists

Rented lists are mailing lists that you must pay to use. Normally you would rent them for a one-time use. There are two categories I break the rented lists into: Compiled Lists and Response Lists.

Out of the 200-million-plus names that I've mailed over the years, over 95 percent of them have been to response-based lists. This section will teach you the difference between a compiled list and a response list and how to effectively pick the right list for your campaign.

Compiled lists are made up of people who generally have a similar interest or relatable characteristic. It could be a group of coin collectors or home improvement enthusiasts or real estate agents or construction workers. These groups have not responded or purchased anything that would normally associate them with one another. Instead, these compiled lists have been assembled using multiple sources, such as warranty cards, government records, corporate reports, telephone directories, Yellow Pages, credit bureaus, etc.

By contrast, the individuals on a response list have made the effort to reply/inquire/order from some offer (they have responded to an offer), unlike the compiled list individuals who have not taken any action and rarely even know they are on such a list. Compiled lists normally generate a much lower response rate than a response list.

Response lists are broken up into five sublist categories: inquiry, controlled circulation, paid circulation, buyers, and attendee.

$ *Inquiry List:* a group of individuals who have inquired about a specific offer. There are many different ways for an inquiry list to be generated. Perhaps they have called after seeing an infomercial on TV and asked for more information. Or the prospect may have mailed in a request for more information from a space ad in a publication. Or the inquiry may have been made online requesting more information about a specific product.

Inquiry lists are generally more responsive than compiled lists because these individuals took some action to respond to a marketing campaign; but they are not as responsive as a list of individuals who have actually paid for a subscription or product.

$ *Controlled Circulation List:* a group of individuals who receive a free subscription to a publication—a magazine, newspaper, or newsletter. These individuals have responded and requested to receive the publication but have not paid anything for it. But they are prequalified by the publication, or they never would have received the free subscription in the first place. Normally, the subscriber has filled out a questionnaire in order to receive a subscription. It asks pointed questions to ensure the potential subscriber is interested in the specific category or has a job function related to the publication.

$ *Paid Circulation List:* individuals who have paid for a subscription to a publication. Lists of names from *Time* magazine, *Newsweek*, and the *Wall Street Journal* are all examples of paid circulation lists. Unlike the controlled circulation lists, these subscribers do not have to be qualified in order to subscribe, but they do have to pay for the subscription. So that makes them a very promising group of prospects.

Benefits of Targeted List Testing

Targeted list testing can be very helpful in allowing you to narrow down a huge universe of names into a more targeted list that will lower your mailing costs while increasing your results. For example, if you are opening a medical clinic for elderly patients and want to let people in your community know about it, you could do one of two things:

1. Send a large mailing to everyone in your community. This would let everyone know, but it could end up being very expensive because your list would be large. And it would not be an efficient way to reach just your target prospects. With a community-wide mailing you would reach a large number of people who would have no interest in coming to your clinic.

—or—

2. Narrow down your mailing list so that you reach only the types of prospects who are likely to use the clinic's services. Since you specialize in adults over the age of 50, those are the people you want to reach. And since your treatments can be expensive and are not necessarily covered by insurance, you'd prefer your patients to be affluent. So, instead of mailing everyone in your community, it would be well worth it to target your list to adults, aged 60-plus, who own their home. This will greatly increase the efficiency of your campaign.

$ *Buyers List:* individuals who have taken the step of paying for a product or service. They have responded to a marketing campaign (direct mail, radio/TV, online, space ad, etc.) and were willing to purchase the offer. Buyers lists usually bring the best response rates of all the response list types.

$ *Attendee List:* a group of individuals who have attended a trade show, conference, seminar, etc. Attendee lists can be made up of paid attendees and no-pay attendees. Obviously, the paid attendees usually respond better than the no-pay.

Note: When you rent or buy a list for your direct-mail campaign, you will want physical addresses. But keep in mind that you can also rent lists with other kinds of contact information that may be suitable to your needs. For example, you can also buy lists with email addresses and phone numbers.

How to Find the Right Mailing List

Right now you may be thinking, "Where will I be able to find all these names, let alone names that are so precisely targeted?"

It's actually pretty easy to get exactly what you need. There are two sources I like to use to help me narrow down my list selection: SRDS, and even better, a great list broker who will do all the researching and negotiating for you.

The Standard Rate and Data (SRDS) Direct Marketing List Source will provide you with an easy and organized way to review many different lists. SRDS will give you complete list rental information (sources, selects, counts, costs, list managers, etc.). It boasts information on more than 100,000 lists. You can use SRDS to search by category, market classification, list title, and just about any other way you want to search for a list. You can reach them by going to its website, SRDS.com.

The most helpful and convenient source for finding the right mailing list is to simply use the services of a great list broker.

A list broker is a direct-marketing professional who can provide you with list recommendations ("List Reco"). A list reco is a group of lists the broker has carefully selected for you to pick from.

For example, let's say you are selling ski equipment through the mail, and you want to reach people who have bought ski equipment in the past. You can request a "list reco" from a list broker who will do the research and then give you an assortment of direct-mail lists that you can choose from, all of them within your niche. In this case, it would be a list of available mailing lists containing the names of people who have purchased ski equipment through the mail.

List Brokers/Managers/Compilers

List brokers have a wealth of knowledge about mailing lists that can make the task of selecting the right list much easier. They can also help you negotiate lower list-rental rates, which is a real benefit since renting lists can be expensive. List brokers offer one-stop shopping for mailing lists, and they will save you time and money.

For example, you can go through a list broker to rent 20 lists or 1,000 lists. Imagine trying to rent 20 lists from 20 different list owners yourself! It would take a lot of time and energy to negotiate with each list owner and make the arrangements for each list to be delivered to the proper location (data processor, printer, mailing facility, etc.). Using a list broker will eliminate the hassle of dealing with numerous list owners.

List brokers can also help set up Net Name Arrangements, which can save you thousands of dollars. A net name arrangement is where the list owner agrees to accept a lower payment based on either a percentage or the actual number of names mailed. For example: Your "net name arrangement" with the list owner could be 85 percent of the names shipped. This means if you ordered 50,000 names, you'd only have to pay for 42,500. Or, sometimes the list owner will allow you to pay for just the actual number of names you sent mail to. If you ordered 50,000 and mailed 41,855, the list owner would charge you only for the 41,855 names mailed.

There are numerous list brokers and managers to choose from, and finding the right one can be crucial to your success. Look for a broker who specializes in your target market. If you have a retail pet shop, find the best broker in that category. If you're selling a health supplement, get the best broker in that category. Also, ask other colleagues in your industry for their recommendation for a great list broker.

Be aware that the world of list brokers itself is broken up into different levels. Altogether, there are four main sources you can go to in order to rent lists: list brokers, list managers, list compilers, and list broker/managers.

1. *List Brokers*. Their basic role is to make arrangements for you, as the list renter, to rent the list from other companies. Normally, a list broker will research lists and segments to identify the ones that will work best for you and what you're trying to accomplish.

2. *List Managers*. They supervise the rental of specific mailing lists that they themselves manage. List managers promote the lists they manage themselves in an effort to get list renters to rent and mail their list. The more people who rent the list, the more revenue is generated for the list manager and list owner.

   They will keep track of all the businesses that have rented the list and what they paid for each usage. They usually ask the prospective list renter to provide a copy of the sales piece they want to mail so that the list manager can determine whether to give approval to rent the list. If the sales piece is too competitive with the list owner's own offer, or if the sales piece might offend the list owner's customers, the list manager may decline rental of the list.

3. *List Compilers*. They manage lists that they have "compiled." As discussed earlier, a compiled list has been assembled using multiple sources, such as warranty cards, government records, corporate reports, telephone directories, Yellow Pages, credit bureaus, etc.

If you wanted this type of list, you could work directly with a list compiler.

4. *List Manager/Broker*. Often, the most versatile source for renting lists is someone who is both a list manager and broker—someone who has experience with both managing and brokering lists. However, some people in the direct-mail community think it's a conflict of interest to provide both services. You can understand why they think so. There could easily be a temptation for the list manager to push his own list over others.

If you decide to use someone who is both a list manager and a broker, keep an eye on the lists that are being recommended. If it looks as though most are lists that the broker is also managing, I'd quickly find a new broker. You want someone who is working for you—and not just working for himself or his company. Good list managers/brokers will provide you with list recommendations that will be the best fit for your offer regardless of whether they manage the list.

List managers/brokers normally make between 10 percent to 20 percent of the list rental cost and are paid by the list owner. This fee is split between the broker who places the order and the list manager who manages the list. If you are a list renter, it will not cost you a dime to use their services.

Finally, when using a list broker, make sure you receive a large number of lists to choose from. For example, if you are mailing an offer for a weight-loss course, your list broker will be providing you with list recommendations from the weight-loss/diet category. If your goal is to rent 10 lists, your broker should not only provide you with 25 or 30 to choose from but also identify which lists he or she thinks will work best.

The Data Card—Your Source for List Information

Now you've got 25 lists, from which you want to select 10. How are you going to know which lists are most likely to be successful? That's where you can turn to a very helpful source with a wealth of valuable information to help you make your decision: the "data cards."

I can't count the number of times people have told me about renting a mailing list that completely bombed. They ended up wasting a small fortune on a mailing that was sent to a group of mysterious prospects—who proved by their lack of response that they had no interest in the product and did not want to buy any of it. Most of the time these marketers didn't even know what the name of the list was. They just found an online list broker and ordered a mailing list through the "Quick and Easy Online Order Form." They selected a specific characteristic, like age or income, but that was it. They knew very little about the rest of the list details.

If you are going to be successful in direct mail, you must learn how to select mailing lists. Your best ally is the "data card," an information sheet created by the list owner or manager that summarizes a specific mailing list's significant details. The broker will give you a data card for each list you're considering using. You should study it well before purchasing any list.

Here's the kind of information you can usually expect to find on a data card:

- $ "Last updated" is the date when the list last added new names to the file. If a list is updated every month, then the "last update" would show when the most recent month was added to the file. "Recency" is one of the critical factors in determining the success potential in a list. We live in a mobile world with people moving around the country like never before. Plus, people's interests change. A young daredevil who buys rock-climbing gear one day could be married six months later, and his rock climbing days are over! You want to make sure you have a list that's updated frequently and that you have been provided with the most recent update. You don't want to send your sales pieces to people who are no longer interested in your product.

- "Date verified" (or date confirmed) is the date when the list was last reviewed. If a list updates only two times per year, the "last update" may be June 2013, but the "date verified" could be September 2013. This would mean that in September of 2013, the company producing the data card reviewed the "last update" and confirmed that it was updated in June 2013.

- Last updated and date verified are important when determining if you should rent a list. If the last update was 12 to 24 months ago, the names on this file are older. In most cases, mailings sent to a file with recent names will outperform mailings sent to a file with older names, assuming the lists are equal in all the other areas, such as category, unit cost, list source, etc.

- "Counts" gives the number of names available for each segment. Here's an example of a list that is updated monthly:

Update	Count
January 2013	15,596
February 2013	17,955
March 2013	14,877

If you are mailing small quantities and don't plan to mail that often, the number of names available on the list isn't an issue. But, if you want to mail often and increase your mail volume, then the count is very important. When picking which lists to rent, make sure to consider what we refer to as the rollout potential.

The rollout potential of a list is the number of names you will have available after you've used a small number of names in your initial test.

Let's say you test 7,000 names off a list that has 50,000 total names available. Your rollout potential would be:

$$50,000 - 7,000 = 43,000 \text{ (rollout)}$$

Most of the time, lists that update monthly have the best rollout potential because they are constantly adding new names to the file. If you test 7,000 names from a list that updates by adding 20,000 names per month, you'll have 240,000 names available to you in the next 12 months.

$ "List cost" is the cost per thousand-rental charge on the list. The list cost will generally range between $70 per thousand to more than $200 per thousand. It all depends on the type of list. A list that is very targeted to a specific category will generally cost more than a list that is more generalized and could be used for many different categories. The additional cost may be well worth it if it means getting a higher response rate that returns your investment many times over.

The initial list cost that's quoted to you is not necessarily the final price. If the base list price is $125 per thousand, there are still a lot of other charges that could be added or subtracted, so you could end up actually paying more—or even less.

For example, publishers and fundraisers often get a lower list cost. If you're marketing for one of these, make sure to ask for special pricing, even if it is not indicated on the data card.

On the other hand, if you have a "lead-generating offer" or "competitive offer," you will most likely have to pay a higher list cost, and you may be declined by some list owners/managers. A lead-generating offer is a promotion that is used to generate leads by almost giving something away—often for free or up to $20. Most list owners will charge you an extra $50 per thousand names rented for a lead-generating offer. If you rent 10,000 names, you'll pay an extra $500 ($50 × 10) on top of your normal list rental fee. List owners will charge you more because they know that you will get a high response rate on your mailing because your offer is low-priced or free.

A competitive offer is an offer that is directly competitive with the list owner's own business. For example, if you are promoting a newsletter that gives advice on picking stocks, and you decide to rent a list of names from a stock advisory newsletter, there's a good chance you'll either be declined (too competitive) or have to pay an additional "competitive offer" fee. This fee is usually around $50 per thousand.

List owners will often request a reciprocal rental from everyone who rents their list. A reciprocal rental is when the list renter agrees to rent their list to the list owner at an agreed price. If the list renter does not want to exchange lists, then the list owner can charge a "nonreciprocal" fee, which can range from a flat fee of $50 to $50 per thousand.

Another cost to be aware of is "run charges." This is a fee that may be charged if you make changes once your order has been processed. For example, if you change the list segment you ordered or want to cancel the list altogether, you may have to pay run charges. The list owner/manager has already invested time in you and perhaps has already prepared the file. It's just good business for him to want to recoup the cost for processing your order.

$ "Unit of sale" is the average amount spent by the individuals on the mailing list (if this list is a "buyers" list). If the mailing list is made up of inquires or is a compiled list, then the unit of sale would be $0.00.

The unit of sale is very important to look at when reviewing a list for rental. Try to find lists that have a comparable unit of sale to your own offer. If your offer is for $97 and one of the lists you mail has a unit of sale for $9.95, you will most likely receive a low response rate for that list. These people are not proven to pay as much as you want them to spend. On the other hand, if you mail a list that has a unit of sale for $195, it should perform well, assuming, of course, that the list is in your target category.

$ "List source" or "media" will let you know how the individuals on the mailing list were generated. There are many ways buyers and inquires can be generated. Here's a list of the main list sources:

- direct-mail–generated or direct-mail sold
- internet-generated
- radio-generated
- TV-generated
- print: classified ad, magazines, newspapers, space ads
- controlled circulation
- attendee
- compiled

The list source will often be derived from more than one medium. For example, one list could be 60 percent direct-mail–generated and 40 percent TV-generated.

The list source is a key ingredient for finding the right mailing list. If you are choosing between a list that has been generated through direct mail and a list that was generated through the internet, the direct-mail–generated list will most likely bring a better response. The individuals on the list have already responded to an offer sent by direct mail once and therefore are more likely to respond again. You know that they open their mail, read it, and respond to an offer if it's attractive enough.

$ "List description" gives a brief summary of the individuals on the list. A data card for a financial list may say something like:

"Buyers who have spent $77 to learn how to make money from their home and secure financial independence. Easy Option Advantage offers revolutionary trading advice in the Options Market. These buyers signed up for an online service that sends out an email two times per week updating them on the recent trade recommendations. This list will work for all financial and opportunity offers. It will also work for health, catalogs, and senior offers."

Keep in mind that it's usually the list owner or manager who writes the list description and are trying to sell you on the idea of renting his list. Don't make your list selection based on just the list description. Make sure to ask questions about the list and find out everything you can about it.

$ "Segments/selections" gives you options for narrowing down a list to the group of people who are most likely to respond. There are segments that deal with the timeframe when the individuals on the list responded.

Depending on how often the list is updated, a few selections that deal with timeframe would be: hotline, monthly, quarterly, and annually. (Hotline names are the most recently updated—usually within the last 30 to 90 days.)

The segment/selections can also be a set of characteristics about the individuals, such as:

· *Gender:* If your offer appeals to women over men, you may want to select "females" on your list order.
· *Unit of Cost:* If the list is made up of Multiple Buyer files, you can specify the dollar amount ($50+ Buyers—Buyers who have spent over $50).
· Region: You can narrow your list down to a specific part of the country using SCF (Sectional Center Facility) Code, ZIP code, state, etc.
· *Address:* Some lists have multiple addresses for their file. You can select "at home address" or "business address."
· *Demographics and Psychographics:* Large lists usually have a lot of information about the names in their file. If they do, they may allow you to select segments based on income, age, hobbies, and interests.
· *Masterfile:* A file that has combined a group of files together. It could be a "health masterfile" that is made of up seven or eight different health offers with different responses (buyers, inquires, subscribers).
· *Actives:* Names that are part of a subscription list, like subscribers to *Time*. When you order actives, the names can

represent a broad range of time. You may get some "Actives" who have just purchased a subscription and you may get some "Actives" who have been subscribing for 10 years.

· *Multiple buyers or Multibuyers:* If the list has grouped more than one set of buyers together in a masterfile, then you may be able to select multibuyers. These are individuals who have purchased more than one product.

· *Enhanced Lists:* These lists have added or appended data to their current file to "enhance" it. Companies with large files do this often so they will know more about their customers. Most enhanced files will give you more demographic and psychographic information to choose from.

When ordering a list for the first time, narrow it down and make it as targeted as possible. Taking extra selections will cost more, but I've always found the boost in response outweighed the extra cost. If the list is a success, the next step is to test it again by removing a segment to see if it will still perform well. You'll want to do this until you find the most efficient segment(s) to take.

$ "Minimum order" is the smallest group of names you can order. Some lists require you to order at least 3,000 names, and others require you to order at least 5,000.

$ "Delivery of the list" is normally very easy, and you have multiple options. You can choose to receive labels with the name and address printed on them, or you can have the file sent via email, CD, or flash drive. You can also ask to have key codes (see below) assigned to the list for you. Each delivery method costs a different fee, and of course, there's a charge for assigning key codes.

$ "Key codes" are identifying codes that you assign to each list so you can track the results of your mail campaign. If you are mailing seven lists, you'll want to assign seven different key codes—one for each list. You can use just about any sequence you want. I like to start with a letter and then add four numbers following it. For example:

W1234	W1236	W1238	W1240
W1235	W1237	W1239	

When the prospect responds to your mailing, you'll immediately want to capture this key code so you will know which list the responder came from. At the end of the campaign, you'll be able see which list performed best based on the key codes. You can use that information to run a more efficient campaign the next time around.

$ "Continuation/usage list" is another valuable resource for determining if you should rent a list or not. Most of the time you have to ask for continuation/usage list information. It's not always on the data card, but it should be. This list will show you which other mailers have used the list. Some list owners will break it up into two groups: those who have tested the list and those who have continued on the list. If you see a mailer that has a similar offer to yours and they have tested but not continued on the list, you may want to stay away from that list. On the other hand, if you see a mailer who has a similar offer to yours and they are on the tested list and the continuation list, chances are that this list is working for them and you should test it yourself.

As you can see, a data card offers a lot of information. You just need to know what to look for. You can find a sample of what a data card looks like at: www.TheDirectMailSolution.com.

After you've selected the lists you want to rent and placed your list orders, you'll have to sign a "list rental agreement" (LRA). This agreement will specify in writing all the details of the arrangement between the list renter and the list owner/manager.

How to Turn a Marginal Mailing List into a Great One

What happens if you mail a list and the results are marginal but not great?

In most cases, you can turn a marginal mailing list into a profitable one by enhancing the list or narrowing down the segment so you more highly target the type of individuals who are your best responders.

Let's say that your primary group of prospects or customers is made up of females over the age of 60. The list you mailed is made up of mostly women, but there are some men on it. Maybe it's 70 percent female and 30 percent male. In order to increase your results, the next time you use the list, you could select only females and narrow down to your best customers.

Or let's say that the list has the option of taking multibuyers, people who have purchased more than one time. The next time you rent the list, you could select the multibuyer segment, so you would mail only to people who have purchased multiple times. These people are more likely to respond, which should help boost your response rate.

Or you could narrow down the list of prospects by age. You could simply add an age selection, and just mail those who are over the age of 60, if that fits your target.

Or, if you really want to narrow down the list and make a marginal list profitable, you could select females, who have purchased more than one time, and are over the age of 60. That way, you're mailing only to the best group of people who would most likely respond to your offer.

Making a marginal list profitable can be fairly easy if the list you are mailing has lots of segments to select from. Here are a few other examples of factors you could use to target your best prospects:

- $ income
- $ net worth
- $ hobbies or interests
- $ geographic location
- $ recency—how long ago they purchased
- $ dollar amount spent—$50+, or $150+, etc.
- $ dwelling type—apartment, house, condo, etc.
- $ product type purchased—books, newsletters, or movies

Whether you can make such a specific selection depends on what the list offers, but you can definitely make a marginal list profitable by narrowing it down or narrowing it down by using selections.

Sometimes these special selections are not on the data card, but if you contact the list owner, there may be more information available than has been reported. That means there may be an opportunity for you to capitalize on those other unpublished enhancements to the list that are valuable to you.

If the list is marginal, ask the list owner for special selects. I've done this many times, which is one of the reasons why I've been able to make lists work that do not work for others.

Getting the best list really is a kind of art. In Chapter 8 we'll look at some additional refinements you can use to get a better list with a higher response rate.

We Know
Where YOU Live

By Dan S. Kennedy

NEVER BEFORE HAS PRIVACY BEEN SO VIOLATED—AND OFFERED up for sacrifice. Online, entities like Facebook trade in information extracted from your conversations with friends, selling it in live time to the highest bidders, and aggregated to any and all purchasers. Your drugstore rewards or discount card moves data about you to countless marketers.

Still, nothing is as precise in targeting known buyers within a product, service, need, desire, or interest as the response lists used for direct mail. You *can* know exactly where your ideal prospective customer, client, patient, or donor lives, and you can go get him!

How to Use Predictive Factors, Mailing Lists, and Direct Mail to Attract Your Ideal Customers

Most business owners are indiscriminate in seeking more customers. This is easy and simple but costly and can, in time, actually cripple a business. It produces a relatively low average customer value—so low that it may make it impossible to do much marketing or to use the best marketing media and methods. It clogs up your business with poor-quality, low-value, poorly retained customers. It puts you in head-to-head competition with all the other indiscriminate marketers, battling for the attention of nominally interested people. If you switch to smart use of predictive factors that pinpoint the most valuable and most likely to respond customers and tailor your message narrowly to them, rather than broadly to everybody with a pulse, you can process fewer leads and customers and end up with the best ones for you. This is the marriage of effectiveness and efficiency.

Consider an auto dealership. With mass advertising, it floods its showroom with 200 prospects on Saturday, who are divvied up at random to the 20 salespeople—whichever salesperson is loose and up next when the next prospect walks in gets him. But only a small number of the 200 prospects are well-qualified, serious, ready-to-buy customers. Most are more casual shoppers. Not all the 20 salespeople are equally skilled either. It's likely two are terrific, as many as eight are good, five are okay, and five are barely hanging on. In this scenario, a top prospect could be matched with the worst salesperson. A prospect with poor credit and casual interest might consume two hours of the best salesperson's time. Another top prospect might be kept waiting and leave while all the salespeople are busy with poor prospects. Imagine if we could bring in only the 40 best prospects and employ only the 10 good salespeople. We would process less but make more money. This is even more critical in a smaller business where the owner-operator is the salesperson, such as in a dental or law practice.

Applied differently to different businesses, this is the idea behind combining the predictive factors of best customers with mailing lists. I'll quickly take you through the top, general predictive factors of response. You have to delve into your own current clientele and current best clientele to look for special predictive factors at play in your business. For example, the sweet spots for highest response to direct mail to divorced women are two months after a divorce in weight loss and four to six months after a divorce for cosmetic dentistry or surgery. In different businesses, I've seen strong biases in best customers for having served in the military; having crew cuts; being long-haul truckers; subscribing to *National Geographic*; political affiliation; a person's or family's name in the business name (Smith Brothers Carpet Cleaning vs. Oak Hill Carpet Cleaning); and on and on and on. I can assure you, there are such biases within your customer base, and they are common specifically among your best customers.

A client I work with in the seminar business recently had a conference attended by nearly 1,000 of his customers. Various products and services were presented and sold during the conference. There was about $1.5 million in sales. Fifty-two of the 1,000 spent between $10,000.00 and $28,000.00, accounting for almost $1 million. In other words, two-thirds of the revenue came from 5 percent of the attendees.

What my client should do is microscopically research, probe, and analyze those 52 buyers. Examine all the information available about them by looking at the 52 websites, sending a survey that appears to be for all customers but is actually constructed and sent only to them (with a $100 bill attached as a thank-you for completing it), even go hide in the bushes and eavesdrop on their dinner table conversations if need be. In earnest, search for any commonality all or most of them share. If they all came from Midwest states, if they all own dogs, if they are all in a certain age range, if they are all politically conservative, if they all engaged in any specific activity or purchasing with the company before this conference, then these commonalities become criteria for selecting prospects to mail to, to acquire new customers, to rule out customers, and to cull mailing lists of people not to mail to. The objective is to get as many new customers as possible who match the factual, demographic, attitudinal, and behavioral profile of these 52 stars—and to bring in fewer customers who don't fit the profile.

You *have* these kinds of predictive factors for your own clientele. But let's back up and look at the top generic predictive factors of response, which you should consider when obtaining mailing lists:

$ **The strongest predictor of buying behavior *is* buying behavior**. There is an important principle to understand: A buyer is a buyer is a buyer. People buy multiple products from multiple merchants in the same category of interest. Not all list owners will rent to direct competitors, but some will. Craig and I both do some pro bono work for a wonderful animal charity, Happy Trails Animal Sanctuary. (http://happytrailsfarm.org). Its leader, Annette Fischer, is an outstanding, self-taught copywriter and a big user of direct mail. In the last year, for the first time, she has begun using response lists with more and more sophistication and better and better results. Happy Trails is a small, local, home-grown sanctuary in northeast Ohio. When Craig went to work renting mailing lists from national animal-related charities, just of donor names in Ohio, some refused due to their view of the direct competition issue. One that said yes was the Doris Day Animal League, and that list provided a very high, first-donation positive return on investment from Happy Trails' mailing to acquire new donors.

There are also buyers of related but noncompetitive subscriptions, products, or services. For example, subscribers to a magazine about fine wines fit with a local restaurant boasting the best wine cellar of any in a 500-mile radius. While the restaurant operator using that list doesn't know for a fact that these people dine out often at fine restaurants, he does know they are interested in fine wines, pay to read about fine wines, and almost certainly spend money on fine wines. This is a big leg up over mailing to any and all homeowners in his area. And it dictates a message matched to these subscribers. The bigger the mailing universe to be tapped, the more you want to drill down to best buyers or buyers currently "in heat," which Craig has written about, in terms of multibuyers, frequency, and recency.

$ **The second strongest predictor of buying behavior is activity behavior.** A golfer is infinitely more likely to buy the new high-tech golf club than a nongolfer. But "golfer" covers a broad spectrum of activity. He may golf four or 40 times a year, play casually or compete in tournaments, play only at home or travel on golf vacations, have taken lessons, subscribe to just one or to four golf magazines. In effect, the higher his passion level and active involvement level, the more likely he is to buy things tied to that category of interest.

$ **The third strongest predictor of buying behavior drops down to demographics**—age, gender, income, net worth, homeowner or renter, married or single. This is not just limited to marketing to consumers; it can apply to B2B, at least to small businesses. As example, I have had two clients, both selling a somewhat similar program to dentists. Early testing revealed a strong bias: The dentists buying were between 50 and 60 years old and were in secondary, suburban markets, not major cities. This information allows reducing the mailing universe by two-thirds, spending more reaching out to only the best prospects, and more directly targeting the message, using age-appropriate photographs and otherwise syncing with the prospect. For a general understanding of the links between demographics and buying, I recommend studying the economist Harry Dent Jr.

I also have two demographic-targeted marketing books, *No B.S. Guide to Marketing to Leading-Edge Boomers and Seniors* and *No B.S. Guide to Marketing to the Affluent*.

Using Predictive Factors to Select and Get Lists

Direct-marketing professionals who are smart (not all are) endeavor to work with as many "knowns" as possible. The longer the list of known facts about best customers and predictive factors of best customers, the better.

Consider this example. A northern Virginia and Washington, D.C.–area matchmaking service, a client of mine, has a bias in its clientele of Kennedy Center members and attendees. They also need relatively affluent and accomplished men, of certain income, who are fit or interested in fitness and/or who travel frequently, and, of course, who are single or divorced. There is some evidence its ideal client is fashion conscious or at least interested in his appearance. There are other knowns that I'm not going to name, but that did govern list search. Figures 7–1 (page 107), 7–2 (page 108), and 7–3 (page 109) are some of the work product regarding available lists gathered for It's Just Lunch by Craig Simpson.

The client can test all these lists separately, segments of these lists separately, or merge-purge and overlay two or three lists and mail only the duplicates. With this, we know where their highest probability prospects live!

And we can go further. We not only know where our target prospect lives, we can know what direct mail he has responded to in comparable product and service categories. Once you know which mailers have been repeatedly using a list, usually on the full data card or data page provided by the list manager, you can utilize the archive service at www.InsideDirectMail.com and get copies of the "control" direct-mail pieces used by those mailers. With thorough examination of the top 10 campaigns being mailed to a list, a picture emerges comprised of commonalities, about the type of appeals, ideas, stories, price points, premiums, etc. the people on this list are most frequently responsive to.

This is a very important point about message. The narrower and tighter your list, the more knowns about the list, the response behavior of the people on the list, and the response triggers used by other mailers

FIGURE 7-1 It's Just Lunch List Opportunities—Page 1 of 3

Lists - Click on list name to view data card	Segment	MALES SCF 200-209; 223-226 Count	FEMALES SCF 200-209; 223-226 Count	Summary Description
Doctors & Lawyers				
DENTISTS AT HOME ADDRESS MAILING LIST	Total File; Age 35-49; Single	36	9	Dentists at Home
DENTISTS AT HOME ADDRESS MAILING LIST	Total File; Age 50-65; Single	41	57	
DOCTORS AT HOME ADDRESS - POSTAL & EMAIL MAILING LIST	Total File; Age 35-49; Single	179	52	Doctors at Home
DOCTORS AT HOME ADDRESS - POSTAL & EMAIL MAILING LIST	Total File; Age 50-65; Single	241	334	
LAWYERS AT HOME ADDRESS MAILING LIST	Age 40-50	255	284	Lawyers at Home
LAWYERS AT HOME ADDRESS MAILING LIST	Age 50-65	374	225	
MEDICAL PROFESSIONALS AT HOME ADDRESS	Age 40-50, Single/Divorced	1,010	2,559	Medical Professionals at Home
MEDICAL PROFESSIONALS AT HOME ADDRESS	Age 50-65, Single/Divorced	1,141	3,243	
Fashion				
BROOKS BROTHERS	12 Month Buyers	6,400		In 1818, Henry Sands Brooks founded Brooks Brothers, the first ready-to-wear fashion emporium in America.
CONDE NAST - ENHANCED DATABASE	Active Subs; Age 35-49; Single	6,195		The Conde Nast Enhanced Database is overlaid with E-Tech and InfoBase Lifestyle data and includes subscribers to Vogue, W, Glamour, Allure, Self, Teen Vogue, GQ, Details, Architectural Digest, Brides, Lucky, Golf Digest, Golf World, Vanity Fair, Bon Appetit, Conde Nast Traveler, Wired, The New Yorker.
CONDE NAST - ENHANCED DATABASE	Active Subs; Age 50-65; Single	5,258		
CONDE NAST - ENHANCED DATABASE	Active Subs; Age 25-39; Single		7,805	
CONDE NAST - ENHANCED DATABASE	Active Subs; Age 40-60; Single		10,742	
ESQUIRE	Active Subs, Age 40-50, Single	352		Published by Hearst Magazines, Esquire is the lifestyle magazine for the sophisticated modern man who strives to lead a richer, fuller, and more meaningful life.
ESQUIRE	Active Subs, Age 50-65, Single	364		
GQ - GENTLEMEN'S QUARTERLY MAGAZINE	Active Subs, Age 40-50, Single	750		Published by Conde Nast. GQ is the authority on men. For over 50 years GQ has been the premier men's magazine, providing definitive coverage of men's style and culture.
GQ - GENTLEMEN'S QUARTERLY MAGAZINE	Active Subs, Age 50-65, Single	625		
PAUL FREDRICK	12 Month Buyers, 40-50	400		Paul Fredrick is a high quality, yet affordable, collection of business and business casual apparel, classically inspired, yet very much of the moment.
PAUL FREDRICK	12 Month Buyers, 50-65	1,000		
VANITY FAIR MAGAZINE	Active Subs, Age 25-40, Single, College Grad		204	Published by Conde Nast. From entertainment to world affairs, business to style, design to society, Vanity Fair is a cultural catalyst—a magazine that provokes and drives the popular dialogue.
VANITY FAIR MAGAZINE	Active Subs, Age 40-60, Single, College Grad		430	
VOGUE MAGAZINE	Active Subs, Age 25-40, Single, College Grad		345	Published by Conde Nast. For over 118 years, Vogue has been America's cultural barometer, putting fashion in the context of the larger world we live in- how we dress, live, socialize; what we eat, listen to, watch; who leads and inspires us.
VOGUE MAGAZINE	Active Subs, Age 40-60, Single College Grad		480	
Financial				
FORBES ENHANCED MASTERFILE	Active Subs, Age 40-50, Single	501	205	Forbes is the magazine that delivers outstanding journalism that makes you smarter, more successful and richer.
FORBES ENHANCED MASTERFILE	Active Subs, Age 50-65, Single	783	320	Forbes is the magazine that delivers outstanding journalism that makes you smarter, more successful and richer.
FORBES ENHANCED MASTERFILE	Active Subs; Single	2,104	1,141	Forbes is the magazine that delivers outstanding journalism that makes you smarter, more successful and richer.
INVESTOR'S BUSINESS DAILY - ENHANCED	Active Subs, Age 40-49, Single	64	13	Investor's Business Daily has enhanced its file with consumer demographic data including age, income, purchase and lifestyle behavior.
INVESTOR'S BUSINESS DAILY - ENHANCED	Active Subs, Age 50-65, Single	122	22	
ROBB REPORT	Active Subs	600	100	Published by CurtCo Media, Robb Report serves the upper class as the ultimate authority on luxurious living, with editorial that invites affluent readers into a world of adventure, excellence, and connoisseurship.
THE ECONOMIST	Active Subs, Age 40-50, Single/Divorced	Pending		Written for senior business, political, and financial decision-makers, The Economist provides authoritative insight on international news, politics, business, finance, current affairs, and science and technology.
THE ECONOMIST	Active Subs, Age 50-65, Single/Divorced	Pending		
THE ECONOMIST	Active Subs, Single/Divorced, Age 25-40, Female	Pending		
THE ECONOMIST	Active Subs, Single/Divorced, Age 40-60, Female	Pending		

to that list, the better we can craft a message with irresistible appeal to that list. One of the many ways businesspeople sabotage their direct-mail efforts is with big, broad, sloppy, one-size-fits-all messages. A fundamental, foundational tenet of all my work is: Message to Market Match.

If the stakes are high enough, we can find a professional copywriter or even an entire marketing team with specific and direct experience in selling to these particular prospects via direct mail, in comparable

FIGURE 7-2 It's Just Lunch List Opportunities—Page 2 of 3

Lists - Click on list name to view data card	Segment	MALES SCF 200-209; 223-226 Count	FEMALES SCF 200-209; 223-226 Count	Summary Description
Health / Fitness				
FORMULA #1 POTENCY BUYERS	12 Month Buyers			Reach male buyers of an all natural male enhancement supplement. Buyers finally found a potency supplement that will revitalize their libido and stamina without any side effects of other potency products.
Health & Gym Club Members - Postal & Email Mailing List	Single Males Age 50-65, Income $100K+			These Active Gym/Health Club Members Are All Self Reported Online Survey Respondents. They Have All Paid To Join A Club And Are Therefore Serious Fitness Enthusiasts.
MEN'S HEALTH MAGAZINE	Age 40-50, Single	1,346		Men's Health, published by Rodale, Inc., is for active, successful, professional men who want greater control over their physical, mental and emotional lives.
MEN'S HEALTH MAGAZINE	Age 50-65, Single	1,375		
MENS FITNESS	Age 35-54; Single	483		Published by American Media Inc. Men's Fitness is the magazine for men who want a fit, healthy and active lifestyle.
MENS FITNESS	Age 45-64, Single	409		
SHAPE	Active Subs, College Grad, Single Age 25-44		215	Published by American Media Inc. Shape, has been and is the leader in women's fitness for over 20 years, and offers readers a complete guide for healthy living.
SHAPE	Active Subs, College Grad, Single, Age 35-64		240	
WOMEN'S HEALTH MAGAZINE	Active Subs, Age 25-40, Single, College Grad		683	
WOMEN'S HEALTH MAGAZINE	Active Subs, Age 40-60, Single, College Grad		529	
Hair Loss				
Prime Health Hair Loss Prevention Product Buyers	Single Males Age 50-65, Income $100K+			Prime Health Hair Loss Prevention Product Buyers List Allows You To Market To Men And Women Who Purchase Products To Slow Or Reduce Hair Loss.
Compiled and Miscellaneous				
ACXIOM INFOBASE	Single/Divorced Males Age 35-49, Income $100K+	35,618		
ACXIOM INFOBASE	Single/Divorced Males Age 50-65, Income $100K+	30,120		
ACXIOM INFOBASE	Single/Divorced Females Age 25-39, Income $100K+, Completed College		5,988	
ACXIOM INFOBASE	Single/Divorced Females Age 40-60, Income $100K+, Completed College		11,334	
HAMMACHER SCHLEMMER MAIL ORDER BUYERS	12 Month Buyers, 35-44, Single	111		Hammacher Schlemmer is famous for introducing new and innovative products that solve everyday problems or enhance their customer's lifestyle.
HAMMACHER SCHLEMMER MAIL ORDER BUYERS	12 Month Buyers; Age 55-64, Single	149		
HERRINGTON CATALOG BUYERS	12 Month Buyers, 40-50, Single	58	93	The Herrington Enthusiast is offered an array of exceptionally engineered accessories for audio, video, motoring, golf , photography, travel and fitness.
HERRINGTON CATALOG BUYERS	12 Month Buyers, 50-65, Single	213	238	
KENNEDY CENTER	12 Month Donors	1,600	1,800	INDIVIDUALS WHO HAVE MADE A DONATION FOR MEMBERSHIP IN THE JOHN F. KENNEDY CENTER FOR THE PERFORMING ARTS OR ITS NATIONAL SYMPHONY ORCHESTRA ASSOCIATION.
WASHINGTONIAN MAGAZINE - ACTIVE U.S. SUBSCRIBERS	Active Subs	20,485	28,551	Washingtonian is a monthly magazine appealing to a well-educated and affluent audience in the Washington, DC metropolitan area.
Real Estate Investors				
Residential Real Estate Investors	Single Males Age 50-65, Income $100K+			Absentee residential real estate owners who own investment property and live elsewhere.
Residential Real Estate Investors	Single Females Age 50-65, Income $100K+			
Adult Magazines				
PENTHOUSE MAGAZINE MASTERFILE	Active Subs	1,420		Penthouse keeps their sophisticated readers both informed and entertained with features such as film reviews, political commentary, wine and spirit recommendations, music profiles and artist interviews across all genres.
PLAYBOY US SUBSCRIBERS	Active Subs, Age 40-50, Single	662		Playboy Magazine is the world's best selling men's monthly magazine.
PLAYBOY US SUBSCRIBERS	Active Subs, Age 50-65, Single	1,038		

product and service categories. I described one place and way to conduct such a search in Chapter 6.

Circumventing Search (Sorry, Google)

Some contemplating all this complexity—which we prefer thinking of as sophistication—will say: Why go through all this when I can just advertise on Google, push up high in organic search, and get people interested in and looking for my products to find me?

Ah, grasshopper, the obvious often hides the truth. Far more opportunity exists in circumventing search than in being fed by it.

FIGURE 7-3 It's Just Lunch List Opportunities—Page 3 of 3

LIKELY / CHECK OFF NOT INSIDE on data card	Segment	MALES BLF 100-103; LEU 270 Count	FEMALES 223-226 Count	Summary Description
Travel				
ACXIOM AIRLINE REWARDS CREDIT CARD USERS	Modeled propensity to use airline mile rewards card; Age 35-49; Single	33,832		Airline Rewards Credit Card Users
ACXIOM AIRLINE REWARDS CREDIT CARD USERS	Modeled propensity to use airline mile rewards card; Age 50-65; Single	30,638		
ACXIOM AIRLINE REWARDS CREDIT CARD USERS	Modeled propensity to use airline mile rewards card; Age 25-39; Single		28,366	
ACXIOM AIRLINE REWARDS CREDIT CARD USERS	Modeled propensity to use airline mile rewards card; Age 40-60; Single		31,707	
CAR AND DRIVER	Active Subs, Age 40-50	1,776		Published by Hearst Magazines, Car and Driver is a leading source of information for auto enthusiasts.
CAR AND DRIVER	Active Subs, Age 50-65	2,699		
CONDE NAST TRAVELER MAGAZINE	Active Subs; Age 35-49; Single	285		Published by Conde Nast. Travel publications often accept free travel and accommodations.
CONDE NAST TRAVELER MAGAZINE	Active Subs; Age 50-65; Single	242		
CONDE NAST TRAVELER MAGAZINE	Active Subs; Age 25-39; Single		359	
CONDE NAST TRAVELER MAGAZINE	Active Subs; Age 40-60; Single		494	
FLYING MAGAZINE	Active Subs	1,300		Flying Magazine, owned by Bonnier Corporation, has been the voice of aviation since Lindbergh departed Roosevelt Field for his historic nonstop transatlantic flight to Paris in 1927.
FREQUENT TRAVELERS - BMI ELITE	Total File; Age 35-49; Single			The Frequent Travelers database consists of consumers who travel for recreation, tourism, research, business, and holidays.
FREQUENT TRAVELERS - BMI ELITE	Total File; Age 50-65; Single			
FREQUENT TRAVELERS - BMI ELITE	Total File; Age 25-39; Single			
FREQUENT TRAVELERS - BMI ELITE	Total File; Age 40-60; Single			
HEMMINGS MOTOR NEWS	Active Subs, Age 35-54 (GENDER NOT SELECTABLE 97% MALES)	1,733		"World's Largest Collector-Car Marketplace" Hemmings Motor News "the bible" of the collector car hobby for over 50 years.
HEMMINGS MOTOR NEWS	Active Subs, Age 45-64 (GENDER NOT SELECTABLE 97% MALES)	1,793		
MAGELLAN'S	12 Month Buyers	1,304	3,569	Magellan's is America's leading source of travel supplies.
PLANE & PILOT MAGAZINE	Active Subs	504		Published by Werner Publishing, Plane & Pilot is the magazine for active piston-engine pilots.
TRAVELSMITH	12 Month Buyers, Age 40-50, Single	50	240	Provides affluent customers with versatile, easy-care clothing for travel, as well as luggage and other travel accessories.
TRAVELSMITH	12 Month Buyers, Age 50-65, Single	190	910	
TRAVELSMITH	12 Month Buyers, Age 25-40, Single	33	155	
Totals		75,879	85,890	

First of all, an enormous amount of selling occurs with people who aren't actively searching for what they buy when their interest is aroused. A person currently patronizing Acme Dry Cleaners is probably not searching online (or elsewhere) for a different dry cleaner, but if that different dry cleaner shows up in that consumer's mailbox, with a good sales letter stirring up dissatisfaction with Acme, making a case for its superior service, advancing a terrific offer, that consumer—who that day hadn't a glimmer of thought about searching for a dry cleaner—can be had.

This is not to suggest you don't want customers who are actively searching. You may, you may not. But if you do, fine. By all means, be where they search, and don't limit that to online. A client of mine, Gardner's Mattress, does very well with a Yellow Pages ad in the Chiropractic section, not the Mattress section. This is called out-of-category advertising, one of many clever place strategies I teach. But you do not want to be dependent on search. You neglect the way most fortunes are made—that is, by circumventing search.

My Titanium Member Nelson Searcy is the nation's number-one advisor to pastors on church marketing. He uses direct mail extensively for his own thriving churches, and he guides more than 3,000 other pastors in doing the same. On pages 113–117 at the end of this chapter, you will see a couple examples of his very effective postcards, and you can see more at www.ChurchLeaderInsights.com. What is extremely effective here is that Nelson is not relying on online search activity to fuel his churches' growth, nor is he mailing a message for those actively looking for a church to attend. To the contrary, he is interesting the "un-churched" with specific subject matter, a description of an appealing experience, a special event or offer. Most, and maybe all, of the people who responded were *not*, on the day or week they received it, searching Google for a nearby church to attend.

Second, the other reason to circumvent search was presented in Chapter 1. The person searching online for anything never finds only you. Instead, he is drawn into a swirling maelstrom of competing options, confusion, and chaos. In my book *No B.S. Trust-Based Marketing*, my co-author Matt Zagula, a top financial advisor and coach to financial advisors, used the product category "Life Insurance" as an example. A Google search offers 189 MILLION resources to study and companies and brokers to consider, including discount brokers and even experts telling consumers not to buy life insurance at all. If a person gets mired in this, he'll be dead long before he buys any life insurance. Even if he roams around a little and checks out 18 or 30 or 50 of these providers, the odds of you getting him are very, very poor.

Third, there is the Google Slap, which Matt also talks about. Google is constantly monkeying around with its algorithms, changing its rules, secretly altering the way it judges your site's content and your Facebook activity, and God only knows what else to determine your ranking and how, when, and how much traffic gets to you. It is actually in control. You aren't. And that's a bad thing. At best, you never get to "set it and forget it"; you must be constantly monkeying, just as it is. This supports an entire industry of SEO (search engine optimization) consultants, service bureaus, and other vendors, and frankly, the field is overrun with charlatans.

Nobody monkeys with direct mail. Everything being revealed to you here about the world of available mailing lists stays pretty static. You can get to "set it and forget it" with a collection of lists that are productive for you, a direct-mail campaign or campaigns in rotation that work with those lists, and a mailing schedule. In the middle of it, the USPS doesn't wake up one morning and decide it's going to deliver blue envelopes this week or deliver your piece only to every fourth name and only deliver somebody else's only to the other three.

The Price, Pain, and Power of Complexity

Everybody lusts for the easy button.

It is a mythical creature.

I now have 40 years' experience building businesses, helping others build businesses, and getting to work intimately with a great number of people who've created extraordinarily successful businesses and companies. I can tell you that far more often than not, success, power in the marketplace, profit, sustainability, and wealth are directly and proportionately linked to the complexity of the business' marketing processes and its owner's willingness to embrace complexity.

To many, this is an unwelcome fact.

As with many things, if you just look at the price tag out of context, the price is too high. What you've been presented with so far and what you are about to be presented with in this book are, at least at first, difficult and complicated—and therefore painful. But if you ask clients like Steve Adams, with 21 thriving pet stores with way above industry average revenue and profit per store; Michael Kimble, who prospered wildly in an industry that suffered mightily in 2009, 2010, and 2011; and Phillis Pilvinis, a high-income financial advisor whose introductory workshops were full while peers struggled with diminished attendance . . . these people will tell you that the price put in context is well worth paying.

Nothing can give you greater, more sustainable, and more reliable competitive advantage than mastery of direct-mail marketing for your business.

Now, more good news/bad news. Using direct mail for customer acquisition requires significant out-of-pocket investment, and none of it is concealed, as it may be with the time costs of online and social media or, for that matter, shoe leather. You write out checks for lists, copywriting, printing, and postage. It's all right there in front of you, in red and white. You may even incur a higher cost per first transaction with direct mail than with some other media, although the overall quality of the customer and long-term or lifetime customer value may be considerably better.

This puts pressure on you to manage your marketing, each lead and customer, and your business as a whole for maximum yield. To leave no dribble of juice in a piece of fruit. Probably to add new steps to your process, new price and offer perambulations to your products and services, new strategies (possibly including continuity or ascension), and new disciplines governing every touch point with a customer where they are won or lost, made more or less valuable. In the next chapter, Craig takes you through many of these back-end opportunities. I also strongly urge getting and reading my book, *No B.S. Guide to Ruthless Management of People and Profits*.

This pressure can be a very positive thing, like the pressure that converts grains of sand to valuable pearls or coal to precious diamonds. It can compel you to build a better business machine, from beginning to end, top to bottom. It can lead you from effort to *organized* effort. It can make you a better manager as well as a better marketer. It can make you rich.

In Figures 7–4, 7–5, 7–6, 7–7, 7–8, and 7–9, you'll see three of Nelson Searcy's very effective church marketing postcards.

FIGURE 7-4 Nelson Financial Peace, front

FIGURE 7-5 Nelson Financial Peace, back

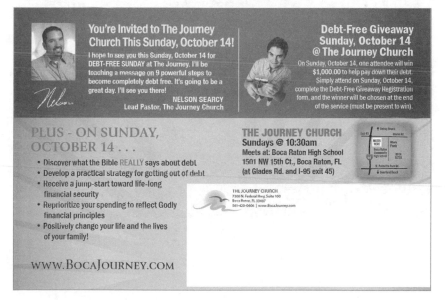

FIGURE 7-6 Nelson Easter, front

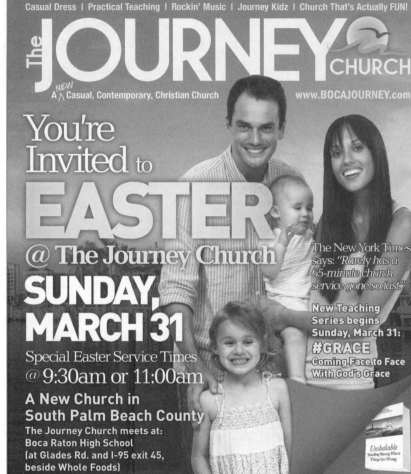

FIGURE 7-7 Nelson Easter, back

FIGURE 7-8 Nelson Tempted Journey, front

FIGURE 7-9 Nelson Tempted Journey, back

Expanding Your Mailing Universe

*I*T'S TIME TO REVISIT YOUR FACE CREAM BUSINESS.

Suppose you've been using direct mail to sell your face cream, and it's been going pretty well. You found a list you like that's updated regularly, and it allows you to mail 10,000 names at a time. Out of those you usually get a 2 percent response rate (which is very good for direct mail). As a result, each time you mail you get about 200 orders. Thanks to those orders your business is growing—but it's growing a little too slowly for your liking.

What if you could expand your mailing universe so you could mail to 100,000 names at a time? That would mean you could get 1,000 orders even if you just got a 1 percent response with each mailing. Your business could grow five times faster!

And that is exactly the way it works. The more you mail—to the right prospects—the more orders you get. It's simple mathematics—and a very easy way to find new customers and grow your business.

But you don't want to mail to just any 100,000 names. The key is to find your most likely customers and mail to them.

Especially in today's economy, most businesses are struggling to find qualified customers, and many are foolishly looking for them through the wrong medium. With direct mail, you can easily expand your pool of prospects/customers. And if you design your mailings correctly, you can do it without compromising your marketing budget.

There are a number of very effective ways to expand your mailing universe. I've outlined my top four suggestions here. I've used each to significantly increase the mailing universe for countless clients.

List Research

I helped one client go from a mailing universe of 20,000 prospects to 850,000 prospects just by analyzing its mailing list. Here's how I did it: I took a deeper look at exactly what type of list was giving the company the best response rate and which lists were a waste of its marketing dollars. Then I found other lists that were similar to those that had already worked for them. I was able to get it a list of names that was both larger and more highly targeted at the same time.

Tens of thousands of lists are available to rent. Knowing the characteristics of your ideal customer will help you do targeted research so you can find the best lists to take. The more you know about your current buyers, the better job you can do at list research and selection. Then you just need to line up your current customers with prospect lists and find the ones that are very similar.

Researching lists is one great way to expand your mailing universe.

Price Test

The second way to expand your mailing universe is to change or modify your price point.

Let's say you're selling something for $97 through the mail. You could change the pricing offer to three payments of $39.95. That may open the door to a new universe of prospects who have not shown a willingness to spend $97 all at once in the past, but who might be willing to make three payments of $39.95.

New Sales Piece Format or Copy

The third way you can expand your universe is by trying to mail a different format/sales package or by revising the sales copy you're currently using. If you are mailing an eight-page letter, try increasing the page count to 16. You may find that you get a higher response rate with a longer sales letter (or a different sales package), allowing you to budget more money to mail to more prospects.

Increase Your Customer Lifetime Value

The fourth way I encourage companies to expand their universe is to try growing the lifetime value of their customers. If each new customer is worth more money to you, you may be willing to spend more money to acquire customers. That means you will be sending out more mailers to a larger mailing universe. This is a very important concept to understand. Using increased lifetime value of the customer to help expand your mailing universe is key to becoming a very successful direct-mail marketer.

For example, let's say that your customer lifetime value is $300 on average—they'll end up spending $300 on your products. Now suppose that through your direct-mail campaign, you spend $175 to acquire each new customer. If your customer lifetime value is $300 and it costs you $175 to get each customer, then you are making $125 for each new customer you acquire. This is a good return on your investment—but let's see how we can improve that.

By paying an acquisition cost of $175, you may be limiting yourself to a smaller mailing universe—but with a lifetime value of $300, that may be all you can afford. But, if you increase the lifetime value of your customer, then you may be willing to spend more to acquire a new customer—which would increase your mailing universe.

So, let's say that you can increase your customer lifetime value to $500. If you can do that, then you may be willing to spend as much as $225 to acquire a customer. How will this impact mail campaigns?

It means that your response rates don't have to be as high because you are willing to pay more for each customer, so maybe you'll be willing to cast a wider net and maybe send a more elaborate package. You can do that because you know you're going to make more off each customer you do get. You know that because your lifetime value is much higher. Let's see how the math works out:

- $ You spend $225 to acquire a customer.
- $ Your lifetime value is $500.
- $ You end up making $275 off of each new customer—more than double what you were making before.

Not only are you making more, but because you are mailing to more prospects, you are also bringing in more customers. This means your overall profits will skyrocket!

I worked with a publisher who thought he had a mailing universe of only 450,000 people. I told him I could help him significantly increase his mailing universe and profits within a few months. He didn't think it was possible. I was able to help him increase his customer lifetime value from $550 to just over $990. I then convinced him that on the basis of that, it would now be worthwhile to increase his cost per acquisition from $220 to $350. Just by increasing the cost per acquisition by $130, we were able to expand the mailing universe by five times! This led to many more orders, and with the increased lifetime value per customer, the company grew quickly.

Increasing your customer's lifetime value can have a huge impact on how much you can expand your mailing universe. One way to increase lifetime value is to get a better calculation of what each customer is actually worth to you. Another way to build lifetime value is to offer additional products or services to customers after their initial purchase. We'll look at how to do that in greater detail later in this chapter.

Increase Lifetime Value by Building an Ongoing Relationship with Your Customers

Let's say you were in the insurance business. If you sold an insurance policy one time for one fee and never saw another dime again from any client, you'd have to sell far too many insurance policies each month to generate a profit.

The reason why insurance companies and agents are so successful is that once clients sign up, they make an insurance payment every month. It's residual income (kind of sounds like multilevel marketing, doesn't it?). The insurance business has a very high customer lifetime value. Each customer pays a monthly fee and often will stay with the same insurance company for years. We can learn a valuable lesson from this.

Lifetime value is a vital part of direct marketing. It's what you can use to calculate profits, determine what your cost per acquisition should be, and analyze what marketing methods work best for you.

Calculating lifetime value is essential for all direct-response companies. However, there are many different views about the best ways to use and calculate lifetime value. I'll give you the basics and then you can modify them to fit your marketing model.

Lifetime value (LTV) can also be referred as customer lifetime value (CLV) or lifetime customer value (LCV). The most commonly used term is just "lifetime value." Lifetime value is the dollar amount the average customer will spend during his or her relationship with your business.

This metric is critical in planning future direct-mail campaigns and projecting profit/losses for current campaigns. Because lifetime value tells you what each customer is worth to your business, you can use this information to better project the outcome of a marketing campaign. You'll know in advance if the campaign is most likely going to generate a profit or a loss. Unfortunately, many companies overlook the significance of determining lifetime value when designing an advertising program.

Let's look at two examples of how lifetime value can greatly impact your outlook for planning a direct-mail campaign.

A Tale of Two Health Clubs

Do you have a membership in a gym or health club? If you do, you know that most of these establishments don't let you pay on a per-visit basis. As soon as you walk through the doors, they get you set up with a contract where you pay an initial membership fee, and then you pay month-by-month dues. This is very sound business sense on their part.

From the club's standpoint, just getting a one-time payment from you isn't enough to keep the business growing. How many people would have to make that one-time payment, and how many new customers would they have to attract, to make any kind of profit?

No, what they want to do is get each customer in a program in which he or she is contracted to pay money month after month after month. Each customer then represents tremendous lifetime value.

But how much is that lifetime value? If the health club calculates lifetime value correctly, it will know how much it can spend to acquire each new customer and run a robust campaign. But if it doesn't, it may underestimate how much each customer is actually worth to them, and this may derail its efforts from the very start. Here are two examples that show how the way a health club calculates lifetime value can make or break its direct-mail campaign.

The Short-Sighted Health Club

A health club wants to promote a new location. It's planning to mail to 10,000 people, offering a one-month trial membership for $39.95 and no commitment, and it wants to estimate the campaign's projected profit/loss. Unfortunately, the marketing person is really just one of the trainers, with no marketing background, and he doesn't understand the concept of lifetime value. Here are the figures he's working with:

Number of pieces mailed: 10,000
Cost of one-month trial membership: $39.95
No lifetime value has been calculated
Cost of mailing (printing, postage, list rental, computer processing, mail processing): $6,000
Estimated response rate: 1 percent, or 100 customers
The estimated profit/loss *without* calculating the lifetime value would be:

> [FOR]100 customers
>> x $39.95 one-month trial membership
>> $3,995 gross
>> $6,000 mail cost
>> ($2,005) loss

Without lifetime value calculated into the campaign, this health club wouldn't want to proceed with the mailing. The projections show it would be a huge loss. So they send a teenager around town putting flyers on car windshields in the rain. And the results are miserable.

The Veteran Marketer Has the Big Picture

This same health club is promoting a new location, but this time the manager has some marketing experience and knows how to use lifetime value to help project the campaign's outcome. The manager knows that people who take the trial, on average, will pay for six months of membership. So let's look at the figures now:

Number of pieces mailed: 10,000
Cost of one-month trial membership: $39.95
Average dues paid over six months: $239.70
Cost of mailing (printing, postage, list rental, computer processing, mail processing): $6,000

Estimated response rate: 1 percent, or 100 customers

The estimated profit/loss with calculating the lifetime value would be:

> [FOR]100 customers
> $39.95 one-month trial membership
> x $239.70 LTV
> $23,970 gross
> – $6,000 mail cost
> $17,970 profit

Adding lifetime value into the equation makes it clear that this can be a highly profitable campaign. If the health club had followed the first example, it probably wouldn't have run the mail campaign and would have missed out on $17,970 in profits!

As you can see, using the lifetime value to calculate an estimated profit/loss for a campaign is critical. If you are not doing this, you are probably missing the boat on a great many marketing opportunities.

Drilling Down to Determine Lifetime Value

A captain of a large ocean liner will often travel with the ocean currents to save time and fuel. In order to find the right path, the captain will use charts and maps to guide him to the most efficient route across the ocean. When we market our businesses, we need to do the same thing. Taking a close look at lifetime value will help guide us in this arena of direct marketing. Using the direct-marketing "charts" and "maps," we'll be able to determine which path is most efficient and profitable.

For example, at first glance $300 may seem like a lot of money to acquire a customer. If you know that your lifetime value is $750, it may look more reasonable. But if your lifetime value is $650, then you may be willing to spend only $250 per new customer. Knowing your lifetime value can be a huge help with planning your direct-mail campaigns. You'll know exactly how much you are willing (and able) to spend to bring in a new customer.

Let's look at an example of how you can calculate your lifetime value. Keep in mind, when you calculate lifetime value, most of the time it is a relative number. It's not an exact figure per customer, but just an average across customers.

Let's say you sell a financial newsletter at $97 per quarter. You know that your average renewal rate per quarter is 80 percent. You also have a seminar you recorded and made into a DVD workshop package that you sell to your subscribers for $295. Through your marketing efforts, you've found that 3 percent of those who sign up for your newsletter will buy the DVD package. Here's how you could quickly calculate your lifetime value:

- 10 subscribers each pay $97 for a three-month subscription = $970
- Eight of the 10 subscribers continue for a second quarter = an additional $776
- Six of the 10 subscribers continue for a third quarter = an additional $582
- Four of the 10 subscribers continue for a fourth quarter = an additional $388
- Three of the 10 also purchase the $295 DVD seminar package = $885
- The total return from the original 10 subscribers would be:

> $970 for first quarter
> $776 for second quarter
> $582 for third quarter
> $388 for fourth quarter
> $885 for DVD package
> $3,601 total return

The average would be $360.10 LTV per person for this particular business model. The formula is easy, but tracking each subscriber is much more complicated. This is also figured on just the gross amount.

Now we'll take it one step further to calculate the lifetime value, this time finding the net amount.

First, we need to take out the costs associated with each product/ service.

> $97 three-month newsletter subscription:
>
> [FOR] $3.25 credit card and bank processing fees
> $3.20 order and renewal processing
> <u>$7.35 newsletter fulfillment cost for three months</u>
> $13.80 product cost

> $97 newsletter subscription sale price:
>
> [FOR] <u>–$13.80 product cost</u>
> $83.20 net profit per order/renewal

> $295 DVD seminar package:
>
> [FOR] $9.90 credit card and bank processing fees
> $3.20 order processing
> $7.80 shipping cost
> <u>$13.50 package fulfillment cost (DVD duplication,</u>
> <u>packaging, printing, etc.)</u>
> $34.40 product cost

> $295 DVD seminar package sale price:
>
> [FOR] <u>–$34.40 product cost</u>
> $260.60 net profit per order

Next, we do the same calculation as before, using the net amounts.

- $ 10 subscribers each pay $97 for a three-month subscription (calculate using net profit number of $83.20) = $832
- $ Eight of the 10 subscribers continue for a second quarter (calculate using net profit number of $83.20) = an additional $665.60
- $ Six of the 10 subscribers continue for a third quarter (calculate using net profit number of $83.20) = an additional $499.20

$ Four of the 10 subscribers continue for a fourth quarter (calculate using net profit number of $83.20) = an additional $332.80

$ Three of the 10 also purchase the $295 DVD seminar package (calculate using net profit number of $260.60) = $781.80

The total return from the original 10 subscribers would be:

$3.20 order processing

[FOR] $832 for first quarter

$665.60 for second quarter

$499.20 for third quarter

$332.80 for fourth quarter

$781.80 for DVD package

$3,111.40 total return

The lifetime value average would be $311.14 net per person for this particular business model.

This calculation is simplified. Your specific business model, customer lifecycle, and the length of time you want to track the lifetime value will change how it's calculated. You need to determine which costs are critical for estimating the success of your campaign.

Issues Concerning Lifetime Value

Some marketers have very strong opinions about how lifetime value should be calculated. There are two main areas of disagreement:

1. Do you calculate lifetime value for the full life of the customer—five or more years—or for a specific time—one, two, or three years?

2. When figuring the lifetime value of a customer, what costs do you take out: just marketing costs and product costs, or company overhead as well—rent, electricity, insurance?

While there are many good arguments that can be made for each approach, I fall in the middle; when companies ask me how long I think they should track lifetime value, I tell them they should at least track it two ways.

Long Term

I suggest tracking the lifetime value for two to three years if it's a product-based business, or three to five years if it's a subscription-based business, like a newsletter or magazine. This long-term calculation will give you good idea of a customer's true lifetime value, but I wouldn't recommend using this number for projecting profitability from a marketing campaign.

Short Term

I also suggest calculating the lifetime value on a much shorter term— nine months to a year. I'd use this number to project profitability for direct-mail campaigns. When planning your marketing campaigns, you don't want to wait two to three years to recoup your marketing costs and make a profit. Most companies would like to recoup their cost and generate a profit within six months to a year. Using short-term lifetime value to evaluate a campaign will help accomplish this.

When deciding whether to use the long- or short-term lifetime value figure, ask yourself, "How long do I want to wait to recoup my costs and start making a profit?"

When it comes to calculating what costs should be taken out of your lifetime value figure, I normally stick with the costs directly associated with the products/services you are selling. Everything that goes into the product or service should be taken out. This may include bank fees, product duplication/printing costs, assembly wages, phone charges, shipping, and so on. If your product requires assembly, like a handmade toy, figure out how much it costs to assemble one toy. If you can assemble 20 toys in an hour, take your hourly wage divided by the number of toys assembled—this will give you your unit cost. Do this with all the items related to the product/service.

I also take out refunds. If you have a refund rate of 10 percent for each product, make sure you account for that when calculating your lifetime value.

How Lifetime Value Can Directly Impact the Size of Your Mail Campaigns

The examples below show that the higher your lifetime value is, the more names you'll be able to mail.

Example 1

In Example 1, with a $100 lifetime value, mailing 500,000 pieces incurs a substantial loss.

Net product price: $56
12-month LTV net: $100

Mail Cost	Number Mailed	Response Rate	Number of Orders	Net Profit /Loss	LTV Profit /Loss
$30,000	50,000	1.%	500	($2,000)	$20,000
$90,000	150,000	0.70%	1,050	($31,200)	$15,000
$300,000	500,000	0.55%	2,750	($146,000)	($25,000)

Example 2

In Example 2, where the lifetime value was $200, the 500,000-piece mailing brought a very substantial profit.

Net product price: $56
12-month LTV net: $200

Mail Cost	Number Mailed	Response Rate	Number of Orders	Net Profit /Loss	LTV Profit /Loss
$30,000	50,000	1.%	500	($2,000)	$70,000
$90,000	150,000	0.70%	1,050	($31,200)	$120,000
$300,000	500,000	0.55%	2,750	($146,000)	$250,000

Normally in direct mail, the more names you send to, the lower your response rate will be. This is because most mailers always select the best names to mail first, and then as they expand their universe to a wide range of lists, they have to take names that are not in the top tier. Obviously, the names that aren't in the top tier won't perform as well.

You can see in Example 1 that the most profitable mailing is the one with the highest response rate. As the response rate drops, so does the profit.

In Example 2, the lifetime value is high enough that you can mail more names and bring in more revenue, even with the lower response rate.

Increasing your lifetime value by just $100 can allow you to mail hundreds of thousands of more names and bring in hundreds of thousands in extra profits!

It's a good idea to be conservative when planning your mail campaigns. I encourage you to use a slightly lower lifetime value than the actual amount in your calculations. If your lifetime value is $495, use $475 only when calculating your projections. And keep in mind that most of the time lifetime value is a relative number.

Expanding Your Lifetime Value

Every new customer you get represents a lot of work and money. But it's well worth it because not only does your customer make that first purchase but he or she is also self-selected to be most likely to make additional purchases.

So once you've made all that effort to find that customer, you want to do everything you can to make the most of this asset. Businesses grow by building on their customer base. Your aim should be to keep adding new customers to a solid base of existing customers who are continually buying more of what you are selling.

So how do you increase lifetime value? How do you get your customers to boost their buying from an average of $100 to an average of $200?

It's really quite easy. Once you bring in new customers, you'll want to do everything you can to keep them a part of your business family. The more products and services you can sell them, the higher their lifetime value will be. The key is to keep offering things that will keep the customer buying.

Here are four things you can do to increase what you offer to customers and reach a higher customer lifetime value.

1. Offer a Continuity/Auto-Bill Renewal Service

In my experience, businesses such as pest-control services with an auto-billing cycle will generate at least an 80 percent renewal rate. This will quickly build lifetime value. And because there is a high renewal rate, it's not necessary to sell as many other products or services to get a higher value from each customer.

For example, let's say 100 people buy your service, and 80 of them renew their subscription for a second round. Out of the 80 second-round renewals, 65 to 70 will usually renew for a third time. You can see how easy it is to build a high LTV with an auto-renewal system. I'm on an auto-payment plan with my local pest control company. It sprays my house/office six times a year on a regular schedule, and it auto-bills me every other month. It makes more money off of me, and I get better service.

2. Offer a Premium Service

A business may offer a standard service and supplement it with a premium service that some customers may be willing to spring for now and then. For example, a car wash may regularly offer a standard wash, inside and out, for $15 or $20. It can also offer a deluxe treatment that includes full detailing, interior shampoo, and exterior hand wash, buff, and wax for $150 or $195. If it's marketed right, 7 percent to 15 percent of customers will take advantage of this option. The premium brings in enough revenue so that it isn't necessary to sell as many to build the company's back-end profit base.

3. Offer Additional Products or Services That Complement Your Core Business

If you don't have a continuity program or a premium service package, you can offer additional products or services to build a great lifetime value.

For example, a dry cleaning business might expand to clean draperies, leather coats, furniture, and even carpets. Or it might rent out carpet-cleaning equipment and sell related supplies. Use your imagination to come up with ideas for back-end products or services that will appeal to your customers.

4. Put Your Customers on a Customer Retention Path

We want each customer to follow a customer retention path as their relationship with the company develops. This is often referred to as a sales funnel. We tell customers what to buy and when by making special offers at specific times after they've purchased something from us.

For example, let's say you have a leather clothing store. A customer walks in and purchases a new leather coat. You offer the leather cleaner and conditioner kit at the time of sale, but the customer declines. You put this type of customer on a retention path and follow up with a series of mailings. This will be a regular reminder of your business, which may keep these people returning to your store and buying.

Here's an example of what such a program might look like:

> *Week 1:* Mail customers a thank-you card for buying and offer two or three tips on making their new leather coat look great for years to come. Keeping it clean and conditioned would be one key tip.
>
> *Week 2:* Send them a postcard offering 10 percent off your cleaning and conditioning treatment. Notice that the prior week, we gave them information on how to keep their leather coat looking good . . . now we are offering the supplies to make it easy.

Week 3: Mail out a brochure with a short letter telling about matching accessories that would go well with their new coat: purse, backpack, wallet, shoes, belt, etc.

Week 4: Send them an invitation-style mailing that invites the customer back into the store for a free cleaning and inspection of their coat. Getting the customer back in the store gives you another opportunity to sell them other products and/or services.

The customer retention path will help keep your customers engaged and coming back for more. It will take some time to test and find the right retention path for your niche, but once you do, it will be very profitable for you.

The longer you keep customers connected to your business, the more money they bring in. Forgetting to keep your current customers a part of the "family" is one of the biggest mistakes made by many businesses. Often, businesses have tunnel vision that focuses on just the first sale, but I find it more profitable to spend time focusing on creating more back-end products.

The efficiency of your back-end campaigns and products/services is the key to increasing the lifetime value of the customers you already have. The more products/services you can offer, the easier it becomes to generate a larger profit with each new customer. Building that customer loyalty is extremely important.

Cost Per Order/Cost Per Acquisition

Chances are that if you are using lifetime value to project profitability for specific marketing campaigns, then you have most likely figured out what you are willing to spend to generate an order. The amount you are willing to spend, or the amount you do spend to generate an order, is called your cost per order (CPO) or cost per acquisition (CPA).

Let's say you sell a health supplement, and each month your customers receive a new 30-day supply. All your subscribers are on an auto-bill system where they are charged $39.95 per month. You want to evaluate whether you should do a direct-mail campaign with a target cost per acquisition of $95. The calculation is simple.

First, you estimate your mail cost. Let's say you want to mail 100,000 pieces, and your mail cost is about $0.60 per piece. This mail cost includes: printing, postage, list rental, computer processing, and mail processing.

You are expecting a response rate of .75 percent—just under 1 percent. This means you'll bring in 750 orders.

To figure out if this campaign is viable using a $95 cost per acquisition, you simply divide the total mail cost by the estimated number of orders.

$$\$60,000 \text{ mail cost}/750 \text{ estimated orders}$$
$$= \$80 \text{ cost per acquisition.}$$

Because your target cost per acquisition is $95, at $80 cost per acquisition this campaign would be a huge success if you reach your estimated number of orders (750).

But let's say you had calculated your target cost per acquisition at only $60 rather than $95. Given an actual campaign cost of $80 cost per acquisition, you wouldn't want to proceed with the campaign.

Building a Customer Model

Building a customer model is another great way to expand your universe of customers. This works best if you are a larger business. If you have a database of 10,000 or more customers, you should consider building a customer model. I've worked with dozens of large companies to build many sophisticated models, but here I'll explain some of the basic steps in building a model. Each model you build will be different because, for example, one model may be based primarily on financial information while another model may be based on demographics. It all depends on the characteristics of the data being used to create the model.

What does it mean to "model" your customers? Simply, it involves finding out everything you can about your existing customers—age, income, hobbies, interests, etc.—and then searching for new customers who look just like them. You can apply the model to new lists and reach customers who are very similar to your existing customers.

In order to build a successful model you need to have a good customer base to start with and to work with a modeling company that has access to a huge number of records. One of my favorite modeling companies with a great database is the Epsilon Total Source file, which has millions of names. Many of the people in the file have responded to a survey or filled out a product registration card (this is called "self-reported data"). There are other good companies out there, including Experian, I-Behavior, and Acxiom.

Do you remember the last time you purchased a refrigerator from Lowe's or Sears? Your package included a product registration card that asked questions about your age, income, and maybe some hobbies or interests. This is the type of data Epsilon collects and adds to its database. The self-reported data has many advantages over the typical compiled data used in modeling.

Your first step is to send your customer file to the company that is building the model. That company will then attempt to find your customers in its file. If you send 10,000 names, there may be 4,000 exact matches. Those names are then researched in the Epsilon database, and you receive a report showing all the demographics and psychographics of those 4,000 customers.

You'll find out what percentage of them like to read books, and how many are into sailing small boats or like to hike. You'll also see their income levels, age ranges, if they have kids and how many, what type of structure they live in, etc.

This data is extremely valuable and will allow you to more effectively market to your customers. Let's say a high percentage said they like to drink fine wine. You could mail a special sales piece that showed a picture of a nice bottle of wine and then comment on fine wines in your sales copy, which will help you better connect to your customers.

Even more important, you could use this information to expand the universe you mail in a campaign to find new customers.

I did a model for a large client who sold books, CDs, and DVDs. I found out that a portion of its customers were interested in photography and developing their own photos. I never knew this about these customers and would have never considered targeting a group of prospects interested in photography. But I used this great data to my advantage when looking for mailing lists to reach new customers. I selected a list of people who had spent money through the mail purchasing do-it-yourself photo-developing kits.

How did this list perform? Excellent! I was able to reach a new universe of prospects by learning more about current customers through modeling.

The most common way to use a model is to apply the characteristics that you learned about your customer to a large file. For example, after doing your model with Epsilon, you could rent other names from their list that match the same characteristics as those of your current customers.

I have mailed millions and millions of modeled names for more than one client—with outstanding success. Modeling your customers can be extremely effective for you as well if you have a large enough customer file.

OK, now we've looked at ways to expand the universe to which you're able to mail—and you're sending out hundreds of thousands of pieces!

The next thing you want to know is whether what you're doing is working. It's time to learn how to track your results so you know if your direct-mail program is on target or needs some tweaking to make the best use of your advertising dollar.

That will be the topic of our next chapter.

The Wise Client

I love working with people who understand direct marketing and lifetime value.

One of my clients is the vice president of business development for a construction company that builds all types of commercial buildings. It has a division that specializes in building and remodeling dental offices in Iowa. This is a rare niche, and you'd have a hard time finding other contractors in Iowa that offer the same level of expertise and service as my client.

This client asked me to help find Iowan dentists who would want his company to build or remodel their offices—a tall order. But I was willing to take on the project because I knew he was a very sharp marketer who understands direct marketing and the value of a customer.

I worked with the copywriter to create a two-step campaign that went to 2,313 dentists. The goal was to get the dentist to call for a free report and CD. Those who called would also start receiving this contractor's monthly newsletter.

The campaign brought in seven responses. Now, you may be thinking, "That's a terrible response rate. Only 0.30 percent of the prospects called in for a free report."

I should also add that we spent months preparing for this campaign. Coming up with the right strategy. Creating the free report and audio CD. And writing the sales copy. A lot was put into this campaign—all for seven responses.

The Wise Client, continued

On the surface this may look like a complete failure.

So, was this campaign really worth it?

Here's an email I received from the client . . .

> "I thought you'd like to know I signed a design agreement last week with one of the doctors that responded to the mailing we did. He's working with us to design and build a new ground-up orthodontic office and plans to include additional space in the same building to add a pediatric dentist within the next year. Gross revenue will likely be $1.4M for this project!" (that "M" stands for "million").

This came within about three months of the mailing. I would have anticipated they would have had to wait at least a year before the first deal came through. I'd say that three months is outstanding! I'm confident that at least two of the other seven responders will sign a deal within the next 24 months.

If my client had gone into this campaign and wanted to get a 1 percent or 2 percent response rate and have 15 percent of those immediately sign up for a remodel or new building, then I would never have agreed to work with him. But, because he's a savvy marketer, he knew that we just needed to get people in the door, and that in time, the prospects would convert—especially since he uses a newsletter to keep in touch with each lead he gets.

How can you apply this to your business? Have a clear understanding of lifetime value. And keep in mind that sometimes

The Wise Client, continued

it takes time to convert your leads into customers. Don't just look at your initial campaign results, but make sure to evaluate the results based on the long-term picture. You may be surprised at how you'll start looking at each lead differently than you did before. Hopefully you'll see dollar signs and hear a cash register ring every time you get a new lead.

Tracking Your Mail Campaign

*O*K, SO YOU JUST SPENT $3,000 ON A DIRECT-MAIL CAMPAIGN. THE pieces are out the door, and you're finished with the whole process. Now it's back to business, just waiting for all those customers to flood into your store or call you on the phone. There's nothing more to do with the mailing, right?

Wrong.

Now comes one of the most critical parts of the entire campaign—assessing the results so you know:

- Was it worth it to spend the $3,000 in the first place?
- Of the two versions of sales pieces you tested, which one did better?
- Which of the two mailing lists you sent to did better?

We're talking about tracking. Tracking your mail campaigns isn't about the past. It's about the future. It's about understanding every element of the mailing you just sent out so that you can refine everything you do for future mailings. That's the only way to systematically get better results as you grow your business.

I can't tell you how many new clients didn't know the results of their direct-mail campaigns before I started working with them. They had a sense that orders picked up after a mailing, but they didn't have any hard data. And maybe they tried several different pieces over the years, but they didn't really know which one did better.

A few years ago I was contacted by a well-known marketer that targeted dentists. The company had tried direct mail a number of times but said it was no longer working.

I asked for all the data relating to the five most recent direct-mail campaigns. After I dug in, I found that it had a few segments that were not only working but working extremely well. The company just had to focus on those segments and drop the ones that didn't respond. It was thrilled when I showed them how it could increase its profits. Unfortunately, it is not uncommon for companies to miss the critical information that tracking could reveal.

Most people are lazy when it comes to tracking their marketing campaigns. Frankly, I don't get it. Why would you spend thousands of dollars on something and then make very little effort to find out if it was successful?

Sometimes a mailing works, sometimes it doesn't. But if you don't know why, you can't use the information to create more effective campaigns. You could waste thousands of dollars on future campaigns, using the same methods and lists that don't work. And even more frustrating, you could fail to use methods and lists that you've already proven to yield the best results—but you haven't done the simple math to see it.

A Scientific Approach

When you track direct mail, or any marketing campaign, you need to become a master of logic. No emotions involved! We collect the data and crunch the numbers, and up comes the answer we need to continue building on our success.

Think of every piece of mail you send out as a seed with the potential to grow you a new customer!

Now, if you were an agricultural researcher who was being paid to grow more abundant crops of carrots, you would be very careful about what you did with your seeds. You would keep very careful records of how the seeds from one batch did compared to seeds from another batch. You'd measure how your seeds did in different kinds of soil or what kind of watering schedule yielded the best results.

You would do all that because it was your job, and your livelihood depended on finding the very best way to grow carrots.

You need to be just as careful about following up on the mailings you send out. You have to know what works and what doesn't when it comes to building your customer base. Accurately tracking the results of your mail campaign plays a critical role in determining the success of your future marketing efforts.

You can never be sloppy with your mailing results. You spend a great deal of money to send out your sales material. You want to learn as much as possible from each campaign so that you can maximize the effectiveness of each mailing.

Careful tracking shows you exactly what works and what doesn't. If you do your tracking properly, and follow up on what you learn, your business will blossom.

It All Starts with a Mailing Code

If you've been in business for a while, you already have customers coming into your store, calling you, or visiting your website regularly.

Now you've sent out a direct-mail campaign, and you want to know whether it increased those numbers. You could figure out your average number of calls and orders for each month for the past year, two years, etc. and then base your answer on the increase from your average. I talk to businesses all the time that track promotions this way. But, how accurate would that be?

Sure, you could try to estimate your mailing results by looking at the increase from your past sales volume, but there could be a number of reasons why orders picked up, like changes in the economy. How do you test the direct result of your mailing?

You need to make sure you have a system in place to track each mail campaign. There are two things you can do to make tracking really easy:

1. Use a dedicated phone line and/or URL/landing page. That way you know that 100 percent of the leads/orders came in from your direct-mail campaign.
2. Put a tracking code or coupon on the mailing piece.

The next step is to collect that information from every customer or order that comes in. Whether it's printed on the coupon or the order form, or an operator requests it when people phone in, get that code every time.

Track the Number of Leads/Orders

Having codes in place is the first step. Then you have to be consistent in collecting them for every lead or sale that comes in response to your campaign. When the campaign is finished, you will, of course, want to know how many leads or orders you received—but there's a great deal of other specific information that will be very valuable. Not only do you need to know the overall response from the mailing but you also need to know how many leads or sales were in response to each mailing list, each segment, and each sales piece, if you are using more than one.

If you are testing the effectiveness of a new sales piece vs. the piece you're currently using—your control piece—you need to know which one performed better and which lists it performed better on.

For example, I have a client who is in the financial/business opportunity niche. The lists I select for this client are either buyers of financial newsletters and courses or individuals who have purchased something relating to starting their own home-based business. For one of our mailings, I tested two sales pieces for the client. I mailed a 16-page letter and a 32-page magalog. The letter was plain, with emphasis on the copy. The magalog looked more like a magazine, with pictures and sidebars.

The letter outperformed the magalog on the financial lists, but the magalog outperformed the letter to the business opportunity lists. Accurate tracking showed me what type of sales piece worked better in each niche. The results allowed me to be more targeted for each list type so I could get the best response.

From then on, I mailed the 16-page letter to just the financial lists and the 32-page magalog to just the business opportunity lists. Using the two formats in their respective niches has proved to be a very successful approach for this client.

This is a great example of how tracking the performance of each sales piece for each list can help you maximize your profit potential.

List Segmentation

In order to properly track each version of the sales piece and each list, it's critical that you do a good job of list segmentation, which is the process of systematically splitting up lists into smaller units to keep track of your different parameters. That's just a fancy way of saying you have to use basic logic to keep all your variables straight.

For example, let's say you have five lists with 10,000 names each, and you want to mail two sales pieces, a 16-page letter and a 32-page magalog. Here's one way you can effectively segment your lists:

16-Page Letter List Segmentation

List	Number of Names	Code Assigned
List #1	5,000	M1000A
List #2	5,000	M1001A
List #3	5,000	M1002A
List #4	5,000	M1003A
List #5	5,000	M1004A

32-Page Magalog List Segmentation

List	Number of Names	Code Assigned
List #1	5,000	M1000B
List #2	5,000	M1001B
List #3	5,000	M1002B
List #4	5,000	M1003B
List #5	5,000	M1004B

In this example, you have two formats that you use on five different lists. That gives you 10 possibilities. You assign a code to each of them.

In the Code Assigned column, the Letter "M" represents your offer (product/service). The number (1000 to 1004) represents the list. And, the last letter (A or B) represents the version of the sales piece (or price, etc.) you are testing. That code is printed on each of the pieces you send out—either as part of the address label or directly on the piece itself.

When orders start coming in, your next step is to determine which of the 10 groups the buyer was in. If buyers return a coupon or order form, you would have the buyer write the code on the form; if the order form is the overleaf of the address panel with the printed code, it will automatically be included. If customers call in their order, the operator just asks for the code.

You would keep track of how many orders came in from each group. After a certain number of days or weeks have passed, you can easily see which of the 10 possibilities brought the best results.

Was the Mailing Worth It?

When tracking the profitability of a direct-mail campaign, you need to make sure that you track all the costs associated with the mailing. That means tracking the cost for each of the following: printing, list rental, data processing, mail processing, and postage. I consider all these costs the "hard costs" associated with the campaign.

If you are directly selling a product, you'll also want to make sure you take out the product cost for each order fulfilled. For example, I did a mailing for a large pet supply store. It wanted to promote a free bag of dog food to attract new customers. The dog food cost $15. The calculations in the mail-tracking report accounted for each order. Even though the new customer received a free bag of dog food, most went on to spend another $35 in the store. I counted $20 in the tracking report for every order received to help determine the actual return.

Taking out the costs associated with the mailing and the product fulfillment cost will help show you the true profit/loss for each mailing. You need these accurate numbers so you can determine your cost per acquisition (CPA) or your cost per inquiry (CPI).

List History

Keeping track of the list history is important for knowing which lists to order in the future. By keeping a list history, you track the performance of one specific list over the course of all the times you've mailed to it.

Let's say you own a car wash and you want to increase the number of clients each month. You decide to offer a 20 percent discount to all new customers. You rent a list of the most recent local "new movers" (people who have recently moved into your area). You find that the campaign is a huge success. The list is updated monthly so you decide to rent the most recent names each month and send them your 20 percent off offer.

When you do this, you'll want to keep track of the "new movers" list history. How did it do when you mailed it in January? How about

February? March? April? May? June? And so on. Watch the response rate. Do you see a lift in response when you mail it in one month vs. another? Do you see a decline in response the more frequently you mail it? Does it give your business a boost in your slow season? Is it worth mailing each month?

Keeping track of list history helps you identify which lists perform consistently well time and time again, which lists are on a downward trend, and whether there are any lists that work better in one season than others.

A few years ago I was mailing for a financial publisher who was selling a course on how to trade commodities. The direct-mail campaigns were doing very well, and I was looking for ways to expand into new niches.

I decided to test a list of farmers, thinking, "They grow corn, soybeans, wheat, etc., so they should be interested in commodities." It sounded like a reasonable test.

So I researched all the farming lists on the market, and I came up with what I thought was the best list. I mailed it and sure enough, the results were outstanding. I continued to mail farming lists for about three more mailings. Each mailing I took one or two additional farming lists until I was mailing about five or six.

They were all working extremely well when—out of the blue—all the farming lists stopped working. I couldn't believe it. Why?

I decided to keep testing in hopes of figuring it out. I started retesting the lists one at a time every few months. Then, once again, they started working again.

By tracking the list history, I was able to figure out exactly why the farming lists stopped working and then started working again. Can you guess what the answer to the mystery was?

It turned out the lists stopped producing orders during the harvest season. How many days a week does a farmer work during the harvest season? Eight days a week! They are always busy! They don't have time to read mail.

The list history showed me that the farming lists gave a great response during the off-season but performed terribly during the harvest season. I would have never known this had I not tracked the history of the list. List history reveals details that help you know the best times to mail to specific lists and when to avoid mailing.

Dig Even Deeper into the Lists You're Buying

There's a great deal more you can find out by studying how your list performs. I always compare the list to how it performed last time, and the time before that, and the time before that, as far back as I have data for it. I monitor my complete history of that list.

Looking at the complete history of the list allows me to see how the list is trending.

- $ Is the list still performing well, and are the results consistent?
- $ Is the list trending up, and are the results getting better each time?
- $ Is the list trending down, and are the results getting worse?

The only way you can see this is by examining the history of the list. So, in order to see a trend, you have to mail the same list over and over. By tracking this history, you can see how a mailing list, and the names included on it, can and will change.

For example, it's not uncommon for me to mail a list with first quarter update, and then a few months later take the same list with a second quarter update. (The quarter represents the time frame when the list owner acquired the prospects on the list. Most lists are updated four times each year.)

The first quarter update may get a marginal response rate, while the second quarter may get an outstanding response rate. If you mailed the same piece to both lists, it may leave some scratching their heads and asking, why did the response jump up like that? Not that an increase in response rate is bad . . . but the same could happen in the other direction, too, and you'd have a significant drop in response.

So why does this happen? Most marketers change the way they offer their products over time. They change price points, sales copy, format, order options, and the way they acquire customers. This changes who lands on their mailing list that they then rent to you.

In one set of list orders, you may get buyers who paid $97 for a specific product or service. In the next set of list orders, you may get a group of buyers who paid only $9.95 for the same product. Which group of buyers will respond better to your offer? Most likely the high-priced buyer.

The constant change in offers by the list owners directly affects your list rental because you may be mailing to a different kind of buyer with each mailing, even though you are taking the same list.

If you are mailing that same list or group of lists over and over, ask your list broker to send an inquiry to the list owner and ask if the offer, sales package, price point, or anything else has changed since you last rented the list. If there are no changes, then you shouldn't see a significant change in results. If the list has changed, then you'll want to retest the list again rather than assume your results will turn out the same. Dig in and research your lists, just as you keep tabs on every other aspect of your mailings.

Lifetime Value

I know I keep harping on lifetime value, but once again I want to look at it, this time from a slightly different angle. It is essential to calculate the lifetime value of the customer in each mailing. This provides a quick way to determine how profitable your mailing will be. Let's say your offer is for an auto repair shop. You offer a discounted oil change for $15.95. You send out a small mailing to 500 prospects. The mailing costs you $250, and you gain 10 new customers. Initially, the numbers do not look good:

[FOR] 10 Customers × $15 = $150 gross

With a cost of $250 to send the mailing out, it looks like you're losing $100. Was this mailing worth it?

Now look at the numbers after taking into account the lifetime value of the average customer . . .

Let's say you've determined that average customers who come in for their first oil change will come back for other auto repair services and spend at least $295 with you sometime in the next 12 months. Knowing the lifetime value will help show you the true profit/loss for your mailing. In this case, your 10 new customers are actually worth $2,950 (10 customers × $295 average LTV) instead of $150. This means your mailing wouldn't lose $100, but instead make you $2,750 over the next 12 months.

If you look only at the return on the initial purchase, you will conclude that your campaign costs outweigh the number of customers who responded. But, if you are willing to look at the campaign with the big picture in mind, lifetime value included, then you may come to a very different conclusion.

Keep in mind, you must track the lifetime value of your customers for all your direct-mail campaigns.

Individual Mailing Totals

Similar to list history, it's important to track individual mailing totals. Don't just look at the final mailing total one time, and then never refer back to it again. Add the results of all the individual mailings to a special spreadsheet, and track the history of all the mailing totals.

Tracking the mailing totals from each mailing in one easy-to-read spreadsheet has helped me find specific dates throughout the year that are very good mail dates as well as dates that I know to avoid.

I encourage many of my clients to mail at the end of December so that the mail arrives in the mailbox around the first of January. This is the time of year when people are making goals and decisions for the new year. This is when people are considering buying a new car, signing up for a health club, starting investing and planning for retirement, purchasing more health insurance, whitening their teeth, and so on. This is a very good time for most offers.

Also, during certain seasons I encourage my clients to avoid mailing. For example, I always try to stay away from mailing in April. Tax time is a tough time of year for most families, and many are not in the buying mood.

Knowing your best mail dates will help you know when to increase mail quantities. And, knowing which mail dates bring you the lowest response rates will help you know when to decrease mail quantities or not mail at all. Keep in mind that the more years of mail history you have to look at, the more valid your results will be.

By comparing mailing totals you may also find that when you mail a certain quantity of pieces, the overall response drops significantly (possibly because you have to dig deeper into older, less responsive lists). Looking at one mailing total in comparison to other mailing totals will give you a quick reference to your overall mailing performance year after year.

If you'd like to see a great example of a mail-tracking report, you can go to www.TheDirectMailSolution.com and download a free example.

You Need a Great Database

All this powerful information about the results of your mailings lies in your database/order management system. In order to properly track your mail campaigns and calculate lifetime value numbers, you need to have easy access to your customer database and be able to manipulate it to find the numbers you need. It is critical to have an efficient database that can help you keep track of your customers and allow you to know what and when they are buying.

New customers must be tracked individually to see whether they continue buying other products or if they just remain a one-time buyer.

How Do You Determine the Best Months to Mail?

There is only one way to know for sure: test. Let's say you are a landscape/yard maintenance business owner. You should run a test mailing in every season to see which months are most responsive and which months are not.

Start with testing a mailing in February, May, August, and November. This is the middle month in each quarter and covers each of the four seasons.

Month	Quantity Mailed
February	5,000
May	5,000
August	5,000
November	5,000

In most cases, you will find that two of the mailings perform much better than the other two. The next step would be to mail larger quantities in the months that had a higher response rate and smaller quantities in the months that had a lower response rate.

You'll also want to expand your mailing by testing other months. You'll test smaller quantities in the months that fall in the quarters that didn't perform as well in your initial test, and larger quantities in months falling in the quarters that performed better.

If February and August were your best months, then the following year's mailings may look like:

Best Months to Mail, *continued*

Month	Quantity Mailed
February	7,500 (higher quantity)
March	5,000 (new test)
May	2,500 (lower quantity)
June	2,500 (new test)
August	7,500 (higher quantity)
September	5,000 (new test)
November	2,500 (lower quantity)
December	2,500 (new test)

Keep increasing the mailing quantity for the months that your mailings do well in and decrease the quantities that your mailings do poorly in. You'll come to a point where there are some months that you will not mail in at all and other months where you aggressively mail.

Your results will tell you what months it is safe to mail in, but you must be sure to compare results side by side. You'll also want to make sure your offer and sales piece are consistent between each mailing or your testing results will be off. For example, you can't compare a postcard mailed in one month with a letter mailed in a different month.

If you want to test different formats or offers, you can split-test each individual mailing. Mail one piece in each of the mailings that is the same (from one mailing to the next), and mail a separate version that tests a different variable in each mailing.

Best Months to Mail, continued

I've spent a number of private consulting days reviewing and analyzing testing variables and mailing seasons. The results are invaluable. It helps trim the fat, focus marketing efforts, and can change the way you do business. All making you much more profitable!

You have to test to make sure you know when the best time of the year is for you to mail. Even though some of your mailings may fail, it's worth sending them out so you can be more effective in your future marketing efforts. A little loss now will help you reap huge rewards in the future!

If they do go on to buy other products, you must keep a close eye on what products/services they are purchasing. Are they buying videos, books, accessories, or a variety of items? Knowing every detail about the buyer will allow you to know where to direct your efforts when it comes to creating and offering new products or adding and perfecting the old ones.

Not only does your database need to give you convenient access to all the information about your customers, it also needs to allow you to accurately track your back-end campaigns as well.

Accurate tracking gives a significant advantage when evaluating campaign results by showing what works and what doesn't. If accurate tracking measures are not in place, you may be sending sales pieces to your prospects for a product they are not likely to purchase. Or you may have a product that is generating so much response that you should continue offering that same product—and perhaps develop variations of it for additional back-end campaigns.

I once worked on a back-end campaign schedule that offered about 11 different products over a period of 17 weeks. There were a few products that it paid (very well) to offer more than one time to the buyer. I received a 6 percent response on the first mailing for an expensive video series, and a 1.5 percent response on the second mailing for the same product. If proper tracking had not been in place, I would never have known that it was profitable to mail this sales piece more than once.

Test the Waters Before You Plunge In!

Direct-mail campaigns can be very expensive. And often you don't really know what will work and what won't before you actually run one. It's a very good idea to start off by testing a small mailing before investing a significant amount of money in a larger campaign.

Start with the right attitude; keep in mind it is just a test. Your goal is not to make millions of dollars off the first campaign. The goal should be to see if your sales copy, format, lists, and offer can generate an acceptable response rate that allows you to expand.

Each mail campaign has a number of parameters, and getting just one of them wrong could ruin the entire campaign. You have to be willing to do more than one test and be committed to testing over and over. I can assure you from the hundreds of millions of dollars I've seen made in direct mail, it's worth the extra effort and testing to make it work!

Even though I'm not a baseball fan (it moves too slow for me . . . sorry baseball fans, I like basketball, soccer, football), I think it's a great example of how direct-mail testing works. The odds of you stepping up to the plate and hitting a grand slam on your first try are very slim. Your chances of a home run are a little better, but not much. Ultimately what you want is a base hit. Once you've gotten a few base hits, then you can try for a home run, and eventually a grand slam.

Keep in mind that there are numerous ways you can improve your response rates, but you must have a starting point. Start small, and slowly increase your mailing size.

The largest mail campaign I've ever done was almost 6 million pieces. It took me years of testing to get to the point where I felt confident enough in the sales piece and the program to send out that many pieces in one mailing.

The size of your first campaign should be based on the size of your niche and the area you are mailing. If you are a large publishing company that is offering a new product in a niche you've been in for a long time, you may want to test as many as 50,000 pieces. But if you are a small regional retail shop mailing into your neighborhood, you may want to test only 1,000 pieces.

You need to test your copy, format, lists, and offer, and know that they are all working before you start expanding your mailing universe and invest significant amounts of money into a larger campaign.

Getting the Most Out of Your Database

Your database holds a wealth of information that you need to develop your business. The key is being able to get that information out. And it hasn't always been that easy to do. I remember when I first started working in the direct-mail business over 15 years ago, we would have to use long complicated SQL sequences to put lists together. (SQL stands for Structured Query Language—a programming language designed specifically to handle data.) The process could take hours. But today, with the right database solution, you can pull out the data you want with a few clicks of your mouse.

Here are examples of two features that your database solution should offer.

Most Out of Your Database, continued

Easy In–Easy Out

A great database will let you enter the information for your prospects and customers in one place rather than having to enter different parts of the system to enter different kinds of names. In conjunction with that, it gives you a very flexible "tagging" (coding) system for your contacts. This allows you to pull extremely targeted lists out of your house file. So entry of data is easy, while pulling data back out is precise.

For example, if you are looking for direct-mail responders who purchased from your test sales piece between March 15 and March 22, you should be able to easily form this list within seconds.

When you are able to pull a targeted list out of your database, you can expect an increase in response. That means you can be more aggressive in your direct-mail campaigns by sending a larger sales package or including more steps in the sequence.

Automated Follow-Up

A great database allows you to automate your follow-up sequence. You can set up automated follow-up campaigns that allow you to send a specific follow-up letter, email, voice broadcast, or live phone call to your prospect or customer on a specific schedule.

For example, you could automate an email for everyone who signs up for your monthly dry cleaning service club. It could say something like, "Thanks for signing up . . . as a bonus for joining our membership, I've put a special package in the mail for you . . . it should arrive any day now."

Most Out of Your Database, continued

Then, you could have another follow-up email that would be sent seven days after sign-up that says something like, "I'm just checking to make sure you received your free bonus gift."

Follow-up sequences have proven to help boost response rates for later campaigns. This boost in response helps increase customer lifetime value.

Finding the Right Database

While the technology to create the perfect database is available, in my experience finding one really great database that does it all can be difficult. Most databases either don't have all the features you need, they're complicated to use and require additional programming to set them up the way you want, or they require the use of a second or third set of software to make them do the tasks you require.

That's why I was excited when, a few years ago, one of my clients introduced me to Infusionsoft, a database company that really understands the needs of direct-response companies. Now I recommend it to all my clients who are in the market for a complete database solution. For information on this excellent software product, visit its website at www. Infusionsoft.com.

Getting Better All the Time

You should always be working to get better at designing and running your direct-mail campaigns.

Sure, one day you may send out a winning campaign that has a huge response. But that doesn't guarantee that you'll keep getting that same response if you keep doing the same thing. And it doesn't mean you can't get an even bigger response by making some small change. If your goal is to make more and more money, your attention should be on creating better and better campaigns.

But you don't want to make random changes. You have to go about it scientifically so you know what your findings mean. Make measurable changes, one at a time, and track whether there's a difference in response rate. The numbers will tell you what works and what doesn't. Then use what you learn from each campaign to make the next one even better.

What Kind of Changes Are We Talking About?

Really, it can be almost anything.

The sales copy. The offer (e.g., price, discount, free trial, bonus gift, etc.). The format (letter in an envelope vs. a magalog). The color of the ink. The way customers are asked to respond (order form vs. call-in only).

The possibilities are endless. And any of them can significantly affect response rate. That means there's lots of opportunity for refining what you do. You probably have an idea of what may be important. Maybe you think lowering the price would make a difference, but you don't know for sure. (In fact, in some cases, I've seen a higher price point bring in more sales. I know it seems counterintuitive, but the numbers don't lie.)

Select what you think may be the most important variables, and design your tests around those.

Segmenting Your List

This is where you have to think logically.

First of all, you have to set up a comparison. So, if you have one sales piece that you're using as your regular piece (your control piece), and you want to see if you do better or worse by changing the price of your product, you want to set up a kind of "experiment." That means you send one group of prospects the control piece and another group of prospects—one that is a close match to the first group—the test piece.

Second, you want to set up your test so that you can clearly see the influence of each thing you're testing. You don't want to test two things at the same time. If you change both the price and the format, and you get a different response, you won't know if it's because of the different price or the different format or both.

That doesn't mean you can't test for more than one variable with one mailing. But to do that you have to properly "segment" your mailing list. That means you have to systematically split up your big list into smaller units that allow you to keep track of the different parameters. In other words, you have to use basic logic to keep all your variables straight, with none overlapping.

Suppose you have a control piece you've used for a while, and you decide to test one different headline. You also decide to test one different offer. Maybe the control piece offers a hand car wash and wax for $179.95, and you want to see if $159.95 is a better price. So you're testing two prices, and you have to be able to look at their influence independent of each other.

Earlier we looked at a simple example where we tested only one variable. Now let's look at a more complicated example. In this case let's say you have five lists with 20,000 names each, and you want to mail two different offers (the control piece offer and the new offer) with two different headlines (the control piece headline with the new headline). Here's one way you can effectively segment your lists:

Offer 1: Headline 1 List Segmentation (Control Piece)

List	Number of Names	Code Assigned
List #1	5,000	M1000AC
List #2	5,000	M1001AC
List #3	5,000	M1002AC
List #4	5,000	M1003AC
List #5	5,000	M1004AC

Offer 1: Headline 2 List Segmentation (Test Piece 1)

List	Number of Names	Code Assigned
List #1	5,000	M1000AD
List #2	5,000	M1001AD
List #3	5,000	M1002AD
List #4	5,000	M1003AD
List #5	5,000	M1004AD

Offer 2: Headline 1 List Segmentation (Test Piece 2)

List	Number of Names	Code Assigned
List #1	5,000	M1000BC
List #2	5,000	M1001BC
List #3	5,000	M1002BC
List #4	5,000	M1003BC
List #5	5,000	M1004BC

Offer 2: Headline 2 List Segmentation (Test Piece 3)

List	Number of Names	Code Assigned
List #1	5,000	M1000BD
List #2	5,000	M1001BD
List #3	5,000	M1002BD
List #4	5,000	M1003BD
List #5	5,000	M1004BD

In this example, you have two offers and two headlines that you use on five different lists. That gives you 20 possibilities. You assign a code to each of those possibilities.

In the Code Assigned column, the letter "M" represents your product. The number (1000 to 1004) represents the list. The next to last letter (A or B) represents the offer you're testing. And the last letter (C or D) represents the headline you're testing. That code is printed on each of the pieces you send out—either as part of the address label, coupon, or directly on the piece itself.

If the control piece gets the best response, you know that Headline 1 and Offer 1 can't be beat by the changes you made. You can forget Headline 2 and Offer 2 and try something else for the next mailing.

If test piece 3 outperforms the control piece, you know it's good, but is it because of Headline 2, Offer 2, or both? We look to our other two pieces to tell us. If Test Piece 1 outperforms the Control Piece we know Headline 2 worked (both pieces had the same offer and only differed in the headline). If Test Piece 2 outperforms the control piece we know that Offer 2 worked (both pieces had the same headline and only differed in the offer). But, if Test Piece 1 bombed, we know that Headline 2 did not work, and the reason Test Piece 3 worked was because of the Offer 2 and not because of the headline. If you had only tested Test Piece 3 against the control piece, you'd never know that.

But because you did things logically, you now have a new, better control piece that uses Headline 1 with Offer 2. Next mailing you can test another variable!

One last note on this: If the control piece is beaten by one of the test pieces, depending on the response, you may want to retest the sales pieces. Mail the control against the test piece that won. That way you can safely confirm the results before rolling out with the new piece.

To make all this work worthwhile, you have to put a system in place to track every response that comes in and which of the 20 groups they fall in. Do this for a certain number of days or weeks, until you feel most of the orders from that mailing have come in. At that point you can easily see which of the 20 possibilities brought the best results—or if there was no difference between the groups.

This is the data you need to ensure that your next mailing does better than the one you just sent out. It's the payoff of the entire operation—and the key to bigger and bigger profits!

I hope you can now see how important it is to properly track your mail campaigns. It doesn't work to send things out willy-nilly. Become a scientific researcher of your mailings, and you will get better and better at it every time you send out a new campaign.

You Need the Numbers

There's only one limit on the number of variables you can test in a mailing, and that's the number of names you have to mail to. Statistics lose their value if they're based on too few numbers. You have to start out with enough names in each cell of your logic table to make your results statistically accurate. I feel comfortable with a minimum of 1,000 names per cell, but 5,000 would be better if you are doing a regional mailing. If you are mailing nationally, I'd like to see the minimum test cell quantity at 7,500; 15,000 would be even better.

If your lists aren't big enough, you should limit the number of variables you're testing so you have an adequate number of names in each cell.

OK, now you've got a plan in place to track your sales pieces as they traverse the nation or just go across town. You're almost ready to drop the mail.

But not quite.

There's a little cleanup work you should do on your mail list to get the best results for your money. That's what we'll look at next.

Technical Details That Help You Create Better Mailings—and Save You Money, Too!

WITH EVERYTHING WE'VE DISCUSSED SO FAR, YOU NOW HAVE A good understanding of the important issues involved in running a direct-mail campaign.

But now we come to some of the finer details that experts know. These are the secrets that will help you get the very most out of every advertising dollar you spend. And that's how you multiply the profit-making potential in every piece of mail you send out.

Cleaning Up Your Mailing List: How Merge Purge and Data Hygiene Can Save You Thousands

Even the best mail list may have duplicate names, old and undeliverable addresses, or some names that you may not want to mail to. By cleaning up the list you can save a great deal of money.

It's like trimming out the weeds so only the good crops are growing in your field, and you're not wasting your water and plant food on something that can't bring you any return.

Most large mailers take advantage of running the processes of "merge purge" and "data hygiene" on their lists. As a result, they often end up saving themselves thousands of dollars. One of my clients recently informed me that by following my advice, it instantly saved $52,000.

Unfortunately, it's usually the small mailers—the ones with the least money to waste—who pass on this vital step when putting together their direct-mail campaigns. But you can use the advanced direct-mail information in this section to keep from throwing away money.

Merge purge and data hygiene are the processes used to clean up your mail file. They will help you limit the number of undeliverable records, take out duplicate records, and suppress records you do not want to mail. The combination of merge purge and proper list hygiene will give you these three main benefits:

1. By reporting the undeliverable names you find, you can get deductions on your rented lists that will lower your list rental cost. You shouldn't have to pay for duplicate records within the same list or records that have invalid address and ZIP code information. A good list broker will deduct these bad records/names from your invoice.

2. The post office doesn't want to deal with undeliverable or returned mailing pieces. That's why discounts on postage are available if you use the tools provided by the Postal Service to clean up and presort your list. It can save you thousands.

3. If you order 10 lists from different companies, each of which is based on the same criteria, there are bound to be some duplicates between the lists. By cleaning up your lists, you eliminate these duplicate records, which saves you money on printing and postage. It will also keep prospects from being annoyed by receiving multiple sales pieces from you.

Quick and Easy $52,000!

My friends Curt Dawn and Kirslt Hegg are savvy direct-mail marketers who've been doing it for a long time. They recently gave me a wonderful testimonial.

> "Craig Simpson has always given us solid advice on direct mail. He recently had us make one change to our direct mail campaigns, and it instantly saved us $52,000!"

This is a real testimonial, and it concerns real money. The simple tip I gave them that could save you thousands, too, is exactly what we're talking about here: Make sure you run a merge purge to eliminate duplicates on every mailing you run.

If you are mailing a list with 5,000 names on it, there is a good chance that there are duplicates on that list. It doesn't matter if it's your house file or a rented list—you must check for duplicates.

It's common for people to rent a list of names and assume that the list manager did his job and sent you a list of names with no duplicates in it. The odds of you receiving a clean list are rare. I bet 98 out of 100 have duplicate names in them.

Let's take this one step further. Let's say you have two different lists—List A and List B. Not only does List A have duplicate names within itself, but there is a very good chance there will be names that are on both List A and List B. If you do not remove the names from one of the lists that are on both lists, then many individuals will receive two sales pieces from you.

Quick and Easy $52,000!, continued

Think about the waste you have if you are mailing the same person the same piece at the same time. If printing and postage is costing you $0.65 per piece and you can cut 500 duplicates, you'll save $325 in printing and postage. If you are doing large mailings and you cut out 5,000 duplicate names, you'll save $3,250.

It's not uncommon to cut 25 percent of the lists, not only because of duplicate names but also bad addresses, incomplete ZIP codes, or to remove existing customers from the mail file. If you are mailing 100,000 pieces and only 75,000 are to people who you should actually mail to, then cutting 25,000 names would save over $15,000 in printing and postage.

Plus, also consider that for every duplicate name, you're not mailing to an actual prospect, so you're possibly losing sales.

So, if you ever think that doing a merge purge is a bit of a hassle and you're tempted to skip it now and then, I hope this story about a $52,000 savings will make you reconsider.

You have many options for how you will run a merge purge. There's software you can buy, you can develop your own software, or you can pay a data processing company to run the merge purge for you.

I prefer to use the professional services of a data-processing company. A good data-processing company will have access to the Postal Service files you need to clean up your list and get postage discounts. It'll also help guide you on what parameters to use when running a merge purge, for example, whether you want it performed at a household level or an individual level, or at a home or business level.

If you are selling tax software designed for small businesses, there may be a huge advantage to specifying the parameters for your merge purge. If you've found from past campaigns that you sell more software packages to small business owners if you mail to their home rather than their business address, you'll want to make sure you reach them at home whenever possible. You can set the merge purge parameters to select the home address for all duplicate records. For example: A duplicate name may have two different addresses.

Simpson's Shoe Repair Store	Simpson's Shoe Repair
Craig Simpson	Craig Simpson
123 Main Street	987 Summer Drive
Any Town, NY 12345	Any Town, NY 12345

One address may appear to be a business location, and the other address may appear to be a home address. If your data processing company is able to distinguish the difference between the two, you would have them keep the "At Home" address. Based on your experience, you should improve your mailing response rate if you are able to get your data-processing company to use this parameter.

Finding Duplicates Across Lists Saves Money on Printing and Postage

If you mail more than one sales piece to the same person in the same mailing, then you're wasting the money spent on printing and postage for the extra piece. Plus, you're not sending to another prospect who might have placed an order. Here's a quick example.

Let's say you sell a limited edition coin to collectors, and you want to do a mailing to 50,000 people. You order 10 lists of 5,000 names each from your list broker, all related to coin collecting. Because all the lists have a common interest, there will be some duplicate names among them. If you mail these lists without a merge purge, you could end up wasting thousands of dollars on extra printing and postage on mailings sent to duplicate names.

There are likely 4,000 to 6,000 duplicate names out of the 50,000 because this is a very targeted mailing. If it costs you $0.60 for every piece you mail, you can easily see how costly duplicate names can be:

$$5,000 \times \$0.60 = \$3,000$$

What Happens to the Duplicate Records/Names?

One of the main purposes of the merge purge is to find duplicates between the files. These duplicate records/names are also called multibuyers or multis.

Multibuyer names usually end up being very responsive. When you are selecting lists to rent for a targeted mailing, the lists usually have something in common with one another. If you are doing a mailing to promote a newsletter on naturopathic medicine, then the lists should all be related to wanting to improve health through natural approaches. This means there will very likely be duplicate names across the lists. Their interest level in this area is so high that they've bought or subscribed to more than one product or service. Therefore, they are more likely to purchase again.

Depending on the size of your mailing, these multibuyers are usually broken down into three groups:

1. *2X Multis:* Duplicate names that are on two lists
2. *3X Multis:* Duplicate names that are on three lists
3. *4X + Multis:* Duplicate names that are on four or more lists

The merge purge will ensure you mail the name only one time even though the name appears on more than one list. But these multis can be very useful to you. Because these names are on more than one list, you've paid for the name more than one time. And because you are just mailing the name one time in your current mailing, you can also mail the name at a later date. Obviously, you'll want to wait a few weeks before re-mailing it—otherwise you defeat the purpose of removing the duplicates from the mail file.

If the multibuyer is a 2X Multi, then you can only remail the same name a second time. If it's a 3X Multi, you can mail the same name three times. A 4X Multi can be mailed up to four times. Always keep some space between mailings. I like to wait at least four weeks before mailing the same name again. Depending on the volume of mail you send out each month, you may want to wait six to eight weeks before re-mailing it.

Interaction Reports

If you use a data-processing company for your merge purge, make sure to ask for the reports from the process. You'll be able to use these to get discounts on your rented lists.

An interaction report, or a match analysis report, shows what occurred in the merge purge. It will show you how lists duplicated with one another, how your suppression file (the list of names you want removed) duplicated with the rented lists, and how other suppression files (like a prison suppression file) affected the merge. Not all data-processing companies offer an interaction report. If your current data-processing company does not offer one, find another company that does. It may call these reports by another name, so ask questions.

Figure 10–1 on page 174 is a simplified example of what to look for in an interaction/match analysis report.

The list name on this interaction report is *Naturopathic Medicine Newsletter*. This interaction report shows how *Naturopathic Medicine Newsletter* duplicated with all the other lists in the table.

To start with, take a look at the suppression files. The customer suppression file had 391 matches/duplicates between the two lists. This means the mailer sent a file of names that it already had in its database and asked to have these names suppressed/removed from the rented lists. This customer suppression file could be a list of previous buyers of the product it is selling or buyers of other products the company has sold, or it could be an inquiry list that it's generated. The bottom line

FIGURE 10-1 Sample Interaction/Match Analysis Report

List Name: *Naturopathic Medicine Newsletter*

Quantity: 14,726

List Code	List Description	Quantity	Matches
0000	Customer Suppress* File	3,816,849	391
0997	Deceased Suppress	4,380,569	159
0998	Prison Suppress	22,448	29
0001	*Naturopathic Med. Ltr.*	14,726	98
0200	*Alternative Health Mag.*	14,073	82
0201	*Alternative Product Byrs*	6,919	31
0202	*Naturopathic Magazine*	4,910	28
0203	*Naturopathic Prdt Byrs*	3,562	17
0204	*Herb Buyers*	6,761	23
0205	*Herb Report Newsletter*	2,333	26
0206	*Healthy Alternatives*	10,092	95
0207	*Healthwise Product Byrs*	14,859	133
0208	*Healthwise Newsletter*	14,566	125

List interacted with 10 lists of 11 main lists with 658 duplicates. (*Suppress is short for suppression.)

is, the mailer doesn't want to spend the money mailing names it already has in its database. In this instance, the 391 matches will save a few hundred dollars on printing and postage.

The deceased suppression file (a file of the deceased) had 159 matches. For obvious reasons, you don't want to mail to the deceased—I've found that they are the least responsive buyers . . .

Last, the prison suppression file had 29 matches. Most companies do not want to waste their money mailing to someone who is in prison and probably don't want or can't buy the product.

Looking at the rented lists, you can see at the top *Naturopathic Medicine Newsletter* is listed and has 98 matches. This means there are 98 duplicate records within the file. You can continue down the list and see how each list "interacted" with *Naturopathic Medicine Newsletter*.

This interaction report is very simplified. This report shows how only one list, *Naturopathic Medicine Newsletter*, interacted with all the others. In a complete interaction report, you'd see this information for each list. If you are mailing only a few lists, the interaction report may only be 10 or 20 pages. If you are mailing to a hundred lists, the interaction report will be hundreds of pages.

Analyzing the interaction report will help you get deductions on your list rental invoices. This interaction report shows us that we will get to deduct 286 names from the *Naturopathic Medicine Newsletter* List invoice.

- $ The deceased suppression file had 159 matches
- $ The prison suppression file had 29 matches
- $ Naturopathic Medicine Newsletter had 98 matches/duplicate records
- $ Total: 286

Most list owners will give you a deduction for these unusable names. If the list rental cost were $125 per thousand, finding these deductions would save you $35.75.

$$286 \text{ names} \times \$0.125 \text{ list cost} = \$35.75:$$

Plus, because you are eliminating these unwanted names, you are also saving on printing and postage:

- $ 286 names × $0.60 printing and postage cost = $171.60
- $ $35.75 list rental savings
- $ $171.60 printing and postage savings
- $ $207.35 total savings for just one list.

That may not sound like a lot, but if you do this for every list, it will quickly add up.

$$10 \text{ lists} \times \$207.35 = \$2,073.50 \text{ savings}$$

Looking at the interaction report with only a few lists will take you less than 10 minutes. Saving $2,073.50 is not bad for 10 minutes of work.

Broker Report

In addition to the interaction report, I like to provide the list broker with a "broker report" that is generated by the data-processing company. A broker report shows the list broker how many names you get to deduct because of bad addresses, bad ZIP codes, etc. It also reports some of the same information that is in the interaction report. Using the two reports together will allow you to claim the most deductions available to you. Figure 10–2 is a sample of a broker report.

You can get a copy of this broker report, along with a few others, at www.TheDirectMailSolution.com.

This is just a simplified version of a broker report. It's best if you work with your data-processing company to create a broker report to your specifications. Use this sample broker report as a starting point. Here's what each column represents:

- $ *Quantity Expected:* The quantity of names you expected to receive from the list broker.
- $ *Quantity Received:* The actual quantity of names the list broker sent.
- $ *Convert Drops:* Invalid addresses. The address could be missing the city or state name or have the incorrect state and ZIP code for a record, etc. Basically, it involves incomplete data.
- $ *M/P Input:* The quantity input in the merge purge.
- $ *ZIP Drops:* Records that were dropped due to special drops in the merge, such as omitting addresses that are located in a region where a hurricane just hit or where the Postal Service is unable to deliver mail.
- $ *Non-Coded Drops:* These are records that do not have the ZIP+4.

FIGURE 10-2 Broker Report

Key Code	List Description	Quantity Expected	Quanity Received	Convert Drops	M/P Input	Zip Drops	Non-Coded Drops	Pander Drops	Deceased Drops	Intra Dupes	M/P Net Output	Broker Deductions	Broker Net
L1000	Naturopathic Medicine Newsletter	15,000	15,000	6	14,726	160	216	391	159	98	13,646	1,030	13,970
L1001	Alternative Health Magazine	15,000	15,003	17	14,073	88	896	381	130	3	13,168	1,515	13,488
L1002	Alternative Heath Product Buyers	7,000	7,003	0	6,919	30	9	403	107	20	5,854	569	6,434
L1003	Naturopathic Magazine	5,000	5,003	0	4,910	29	20	232	93	10	4,184	384	4,619
L1004	Naturopathic Product Buyers	5,000	3,622	22	3,562	20	33	137	11	35	3,331	258	3,364
L1005	Herb Buyers	7,000	7,003	0	6,761	26	3	160	133	9	6,300	331	6,672
L1006	Herb Report Newsletter	2,300	2,349	1	2,333	15	15	22	6	11	2,266	70	2,279
L1007	Healthy Alternatives Newsletter	10,000	10,558	265	10,092	97	124	399	21	160	9,130	1,066	9,492
L1008	Healthwise Product Buyers	15,000	15,003	18	14,859	90	97	602	212	23	13,055	1,042	13,961
L1009	Healthwise Newsletter	15,000	15,003	1	14,566	84	242	137	210	100	13,544	774	14,229
	Totals	96,300	95,547	330	92,801	639	1,655	2,864	1,082	469	84,478	7,039	88,508

- $ *Pander Drop:* Takes out all names that are on the DMA Preference File (Do Not Mail List). All mailers are encouraged to use this list, and companies who are a member of the Direct Marketing Association are required to use this list. There is no use mailing to people who do not want to be mailed to.
- $ *Deceased Drops:* Takes out names of those who are deceased.
- $ *Intra Dupes:* Duplicate records within the same file.

$ *M/P Output:* The net names you are left with after the merge purge.

$ *Broker Deductions:* These are the names you get credit for from your list broker. You don't have to pay for names with bad addresses, intra dupes, etc.

$ *Broker Net:* This is number of names your list broker should bill you for on the list invoices.

The broker report should be used in conjunction with the interaction report. The two reports will help you get the most deductions from your list broker.

More on Data Hygiene

The Postal Service offers some great tools and files to help you ensure you have the most up-to-date addresses. Here are a few of the files the Postal Service has available:

$ *National Change of Address (NCOA) File:* A list of people who have moved within the last three years. Running the NCOA list against your mail file will help ensure that you have the correct address for anyone on the mail file that has recently moved.

$ *Locatable Address Conversion System (LACS):* Will convert rural-style addresses (nonstandard) to city-style addresses (standard). This will help increase the deliverability of your mail.

$ *Coding Accuracy Support System (CASS):* Helps mailers improve the accuracy of delivery. This software will identify and correct bad addresses to the carrier route, five-digit zip, ZIP +4, and delivery point codes. In addition to improving your delivery, the CASS system will help you receive an automatic discount on your postage.

Make sure your data-processing company has access to these files because the Postal Service does not make them available to everyone.

Getting all the postage deductions available for your mail piece will save you thousands of dollars. You must plan in advance to make sure you run the address hygiene process correctly. Proper list hygiene will lower the number of "nixie" records—incorrect or undeliverable records.

There also are other address correction files and mailing enhancement tools available. For example, some data-processing companies have tools that append apartment numbers to records that don't have an apartment number but should. Ask your data-processing company what options it has available to help clean up your mail file.

More on Suppression Files

Suppression files are lists of names/addresses that you do not want to mail to. If you are trying to generate new leads, you will not want to mail to the names you already have in your database. These names are often referred to as your house file or customer file. You'll need to send this file to the data-processing company and ask them to "suppress" these names from your mailing. Your data-processing company will probably refer to this file as house suppression file or customer suppression file.

You also don't want to mail to anyone who is in prison or deceased. And it's not just to save money. If you mail to someone who is deceased, it could be disturbing to the family, or at the very least an annoyance. And it can make you appear uncaring and sloppy. And prison inmates are likely not allowed to order what you're selling.

Now, perhaps you think you would never do that. But don't be so sure. The Direct Marketing Association (DMA) estimates that every year, 22 million pieces are sent to people who are deceased. And many millions are sent to prisoners.

The fact is, you don't always know for sure what kind of names are on the mailing list you purchase or rent. Of course, you must always ask your list broker or the company itself for assurance that it cleaned the list of unwanted names. And any reputable list rental company will try to stay on top of these issues. But people's situations are always changing, and a list that was compiled even three months ago may contain names that would be better suppressed.

And there's always the possibility that the list rental company did not do a recent or thorough search. To be safe you should always check the file yourself. One excellent place to start is with DMA, which offers two suppression files: a recently recorded deceased file and a state and federal prison file.

The recently recorded deceased file (RRDF) contains data on millions of recorded deaths over the last 12 months. It is updated monthly and includes names from several sources, including the DMA's deceased do not contact (DDNC) list, which is a long-term list.

Both the RRDF and the DDNC are subscription services, and it probably isn't going to be worth it to you to pay the yearly fee, especially if you're a small company and don't mail to that many names. In that case, you can go through a list hygiene service, which we'll discuss shortly.

DMA's state and federal prison file contains approximately 2,000 addresses of federal and state prisons and correctional facilities. You would clean your mailing list by removing the names of any individual whose address matches one of the addresses on the list. The file is updated three times each year. Again, you don't need to buy this list yourself if your list hygiene service subscribes.

While you need to keep your mailing lists clean by suppressing unwanted names, you do not have to subscribe to the necessary lists or do the cleanup yourself. Your data-processing company should provide a list hygiene service.

If you are mailing frequently—weekly or monthly—you may want to consider suppressing your prior mail file. When you are mailing often, there's a good possibility that you will mail to the same person two or three times a year. It's okay to do this, but you want to make sure you don't mail to this same person three times within a few weeks. In order to prevent this, have your data-processing company suppress your prior mailings.

Please note: Obviously there are times when you do want to mail to the same person more than one time within a short period of time, but as a general rule for attaining new buyers/leads, you'll want to suppress your prior mailing.

And there may be some people on your list who have written, called, or emailed to say "Do not send me any more mail." You must immediately remove their names from your list. If you send anything, you'll just antagonize them. If they get mad enough at you, they may contact the Federal Trade Commission or the Better Business Bureau to report you, and you don't want that kind of attention. Plus, mailing to them is a waste of money.

Have your mailing list set up so that you can quickly go in and remove unwanted names. Develop your own "do not mail" list. That will work for mailings from your house file, but don't stop there. Those same names could very well pop up on the lists of names you buy or rent from other companies. So check all lists against your company's own suppression file of people who have requested not to hear from you.

Last, it's very important that you suppress the DMA preference file. This is a national file of people who have said, "Do Not Mail to Me." Sending these people mail will only make them mad and possibly get you in trouble. The only kind of response you'll get from them is an angry one. Make sure to suppress this list from all mailings!

Post Merge-Purge Production

After the data hygiene has been completed and the merge purge has been run, you can start working on the post merge-purge production—the final touches you will put on your list. At this point, you can add in your decoy list or seed list and assign your key codes and splits.

The decoy or seed list is the group of names and addresses you use to track the delivery of the mailing. It's how you will know for sure that your mail has been delivered and isn't sitting in trays in a warehouse somewhere.

If you're doing a national mailing, make sure you insert seed names in every part of the country. If the mailing is being sent from Los

Angeles, you'll want to know when your sales pieces are delivered in San Francisco, Chicago, New York, and places in between.

You probably don't have friends in all those places to send your mail to, but there are services available whose job is to help track your mail for you. Two of the best are US Monitor and Track My Mail. Each has its own way of tracking a mail campaign, and both can provide excellent delivery information.

The last step is assigning your key codes or mailing codes and splitting the lists into segments if you are doing any testing on different features of your mailing. For instructions on how to do that, please look back at Chapter 6, which covers list segmentation.

A Little Bit More about Testing Variables

There are countless variables that you can test when doing direct mail. The simple and obvious ones that most people know about would involve testing different kinds of sales copy, headlines, price points, and design formats. But there are also more subtle things you can test like:

- $ The color scheme for the sales package: whether you print in black and white, four-color, or two-color—and if it's two-color, whether the second color is red or blue
- $ The offer, whether it's different price points, or testing a free offer
- $ The way the order form is presented
- $ Bonus items, guarantees, and coupons
- $ Whether response involves going to a website or calling an 800 number

There are literally hundreds of thousands of different variables you can test, and every test can be important.

As we mentioned earlier, it is critical that you test only one variable per sales package at a time. For example, let's say you want to test two different offers and two different postcard colors. You could not do the test effectively in the example below:

$ Yellow Postcard with Offer A

$ White Postcard with Offer B

There are too many variables represented in each piece to be able to determine which one variable worked best and how they may have interacted. If the yellow postcard worked better, you would not know if it was the yellow part of the postcard or the offer part of the postcard that made it work better.

Here's how the test should be set up:

$ Yellow Postcard with Offer A

$ Yellow Postcard with Offer B

$ White Postcard with Offer A

$ White Postcard with Offer B

This example has all the areas covered. You'll know exactly which offer and postcard color worked best once the campaign is complete.

You must be very cautious when you test. By testing only one variable at a time (per package) you can scientifically monitor and know your results are valid.

As I was writing this section on testing, I was interrupted by a client who was confused by some recent mailing results. His mailing two months ago had outstanding results, but his mailing three weeks ago was not performing well at all. The same sales piece was used for both, so he expected a similar response.

I agreed that the response should be similar, but after asking a series of questions, I found out that he had changed the way he mailed the sales package. He segmented out different parts of the country and mailed some pieces via first-class mail and some via bulk mail. The mailings also didn't go out on the same day . . . he mailed the pieces over the course of a few weeks.

What problems did he create for himself by doing this?

$ He originally mailed the package first class—which in my experience always brings a higher response rate, even though it doesn't always offset the extra cost. In his second mailing, he mailed a portion of his pieces bulk. I'm certain this caused a partial drop in response rate.

$ He also picked which sections of the country should get first-class mail and which areas should get bulk mail. His most responsive state in the past was California, where he was located. He decided to mail all of the California names via bulk mail since he figured the delivery time would still be fairly quick because it was local. Basically, he took his highest responding market and mailed to it using the least responsive method.

This client learned an important lesson the hard way: Don't make arbitrary changes in your mailing, and don't mix up your variables. If you do, you may not be able to assess the effect on your results. Make sure to plan out each mail test so you know exactly how each element could impact your current campaign. That way you can use your results to guide you in future campaigns.

Working with the Postal Service

Working with the Postal Service is a key part of being a direct mailer. You want to have a good relationship with your post office and stay abreast of current guidelines.

The Postal Service revises and changes guidelines constantly throughout the year. It seems there's always a new procedure, rate, or form being implemented. If you are going to be in the direct-mail business, you need to establish a good relationship with a Postal Service representative in your local area—someone you can actually talk to, someone you can sit down with in your office or go visit at the post office. You want to be able to show this person what you want to mail and ask:

$ Is this format acceptable?

$ How much will the postage be?

You would be surprised at the different kinds of things that you can send through the mail. A knowledgeable representative can help guide you, giving you the freedom to be super creative with your direct-mail campaigns.

Did you know that you can mail:

coconuts	bottles
wooden postcards	trash cans
boomerangs	bank bags
metal postcards	and many other unique items

You will never know what you can and can't mail without consulting a good Postal Service rep.

Make sure you choose a representative who wants to be your advocate—who wants to see you send lots of mail. I've come across many postal representatives who seemed uninterested in my business. Even though I told them I could put millions of pieces of mail through their post office every year . . . they still did nothing to help me and improve the status of their facility. (More mail volume would make their post office look better and get more resources.)

That said, I must add that I believe the Postal Service has unfairly gotten a bad rap over the years. Sometimes people complain about delivery or about how difficult it is to work with people there. But, in reality they do an exceptional job. Think about how rarely you don't get your mail or learn that something you mailed wasn't delivered. The post office has a very high delivery rate.

I'm very confident in the Postal Service's ability to deliver mail. But I'm not confident in all the USPS representatives—so make sure you find a good one!

So get on the same team as the Postal Service and work together. Ask your representative questions, and always, always make sure that you're constantly checking the guidelines. I would hate to hear about you printing 10,000 pieces and then finding out that the format that you printed in is unacceptable, or the postage rate has changed and it's going to be twice as expensive as you originally thought.

The way to prevent costly mistakes like these is to check with your postal representative ahead of time whenever you print something that is going to be put in the mail.

Using a Mail-Processing Facility

Early in my career I worked for Ken Roberts, who was one of the largest financial direct mailers in the country. We sold hundreds of thousands of courses on commodity trading. And I mailed out millions of sales pieces every year to sell them.

Ken didn't start off mailing millions of pieces. He started out as a one-man operation and loved telling stories about how at the beginning, he'd get his kids to help him stuff his sales pieces into envelopes and slap on the stamps. They'd work around the kitchen table, and he paid the budding entrepreneurs a couple of bucks for helping him out.

But soon Ken's company got too big for his kids to handle the volume, and he engaged a professional mail facility to prepare and mail his sales pieces. The mail facility would receive the sales pieces from the printer and label, sort, bundle, and deliver the finished mail packages to the post office, ready to be distributed across the nation.

If you're past the stage where your kids can process your mailings around the kitchen table, it's time for you to look into hiring the services of a mail-processing facility, too.

Probably the easiest way to find a mailing facility is to ask your print shop to recommend one. Or you can look in your local Yellow Pages. You'll also often find that many printers have the capability to process mail.

A mailing facility doesn't have to be located close to you. It could be in the next state, or even across the country. You can turn to the Direct Marketing Association to help you find one. Visit its website at www. the-dma.org, and search its vendor list.

Even if you find a company that's located far from you, it's still a good idea to establish a personal relationship. Talk to its representatives on the phone, or even visit the operation and watch it process mail. You want it to be organized, clean, and responsive to your needs. Closely check and monitor this facility, and make sure it is a legitimate company.

Your mailing facility will probably be able to take your entire job from start to finish. You supply (or pay for) the raw materials: the printed pieces, envelopes, order forms—whatever is needed. The mail facility takes it from there, helping you prepare and clean your mail list, presorting your mail, assembling the pieces, and bundling them according to post office regulations.

Direct-Mail Facts and Figures

- According to the American Catalog Mailers Association, up to 12.5 billion catalogs were mailed in 2012. On average, those who receive at least a catalog in the mail spent 28 percent more on items than those who did not receive a catalog.

- A recent study showed that 98 percent of consumers retrieve mail from the mailbox the day it is delivered, and 77 percent sort through it immediately.

- The Postal Service delivers to 152 million businesses and households each day, six days per week. In comparison, UPS delivers to 8 million addresses daily, while FedEx serves even fewer.

- Advertising mail accounted for $16.4 billion in revenue for the Postal Service in 2012.

In some cases you will pay for your postage through the mail-processing facility. When you send a check for postage that amounts to thousands of dollars, make sure that postage is being processed properly and that you are getting what you're paying for. Always make a postage check out to the U.S. Postmaster—so that only the post office can deposit it—and not to the mailing facility itself. If you make it out to the mailing facility, it can cash the check and then tell you it's buying postage with it—but you don't know for sure that all that money is going for that purpose.

For all mailings, make sure you get verification from the USPS that it received your mailing along with confirmation of the amount of postage used. If you spent $2,528.35 on postage, get a form/receipt from the USPS showing what was received, when the mailing entered in the mail stream, and how much it cost. Request verification from the USPS whenever you or your mailing facility drops off your mail.

Huge Postage Discounts That Can Save You Thousands!

Check with your Postal Service representative whenever you are mailing more than 500 pieces of mail at one time. You may qualify for a presorted mail discount. This discount can be used for both first-class and bulk mail and will vary between classes of mail.

The USPS offers discounts when you presort your mail because it helps reduce the work on its end. By presorting your mail, you are arranging it by ZIP code and then putting it in mail trays or mailbags. All the USPS has to do is throw it on the right truck going to the specific location that you've indicated on the tray or bag. Your local USPS representative can help direct you to the most efficient way, using software, to presort your mail.

If you do not presort your mail, then the USPS has to sort and bag or tray the mail for you—which takes time and money.

So doing it yourself will provide you huge savings. Let's say you are mailing 10,000 letters via first-class mail. Typically, the full postage rate is about $0.06 per piece higher than the presorted rate. If you presort your mail, you may end up saving $600.

Presorting your mail will not increase the time it takes for delivery. On the contrary, in many cases it shortens the delivery time because one step in the process has been removed.

First-Class vs. Bulk Mail: Which Class of Mail Should I Use?

Are you better off sending your mail first class or bulk? Here are a few things to consider.

Mail first class when . . .

1. You are mailing time-sensitive material, for example, sending a birthday promotion that is going to all your clients or prospects that have a birthday within the next two weeks.
2. You have an offer end date or "deadline" for responses.
3. You need fast response. Do you want to measure the mailing response as soon as possible so you can get another mailing out quickly? For quick response, mail first class.

Mail bulk mail when . . .

1. You have time to wait for responses. You have a consistent mailing system in place, and it doesn't matter if the responses come in weeks after you mail.
2. You are mailing a thick or heavy sales piece. I've had clients who mail sales pieces that are up to 88 pages. First class will cost three times as much as bulk mail. If your mail piece is too large, then the only economical way to mail it is bulk.

There is usually a huge price difference between first-class and bulk mail rates. The difference between a letter presorted first class and the bulk mail rate for the same letter can be as high as $0.20 per piece. That's can be a huge savings! But you do sacrifice delivery time.

Consider the following postal rates as of this writing):

10,000 pieces of mail via first-class mail
@ $0.46 per piece = $4,600

vs

10,000 pieces of mail via bulk mail @ $0.26 per piece = $2,600

To offset the higher postage cost, the pieces mailed via first class must generate at least $2,000 more revenue than the bulk mail pieces.

If you are offering a $39.95 auto inspection, you'll need to generate 50 more inspections from the piece that you mailed via first class.

There are many occasions when the cost of first class will easily offset the high cost and make it worth paying more for your mailing. This is something that must be tested and is different for every niche.

Returned mail is another major difference between first-class and bulk mail. If a mail piece sent first class is not deliverable, it will be sent back to you. If you use bulk mail and the piece is not deliverable, it will be discarded. Only by mailing first class will you be able to track how many pieces were not delivered.

Here are some helpful tips for mailing first-class vs. bulk mail.

- $ Always mail postcards presorted first class. Even if you have time on your side and you don't need the response right away, it's always worth mailing a postcard first class. Every time I've tested this, I always find that the first-class postcards will get a higher response rate—high enough to offset the extra cost.
- $ Whenever mailing a digest sales piece, use bulk mail. I've never found it to be cost effective to mail a digest sales piece first class. The slight increase in response does not offset the extra cost.
- $ Send an invitation sales piece first class; you will get the highest response rate by mailing it normal first class, not pre-sorted, with a unique, live stamp.
- $ I've never received consistent results on envelope packages, which is a standard mail package with an outer envelope, letter, order form and maybe a few other components. Some packages

do well with first class and others are more profitable to mail bulk mail. You'll have to test this one on your own.

Use these general guidelines as a starting point for your own mailings. In my experience they work. But also be willing to test and track your own results. And never assume that saving money is always more profitable in the long run, or that spending more money always brings a better outcome.

Making Sure Your Mail Is Delivered

If you are sending large national mailings in which you are reaching more than one region, you will want to use a mail-tracking service. For example, if you're in Los Angeles and you are sending a national mail campaign, how are you going to know when the mail is delivered? Will you know if the mail is damaged or not? When did the mail arrive in Dallas, Boston, Chicago, or New York?

In order for you to find out how your mail is being delivered and what condition it's in when it arrives, you'll need to use a tracking service.

There are two mail-tracking services I recommend. The first is US Monitor. It will provide you a list of addresses throughout the United States (or specific to any region you are mailing). You can use these addresses as "seed" addresses. By adding these addresses into your mailing file, US Monitor can track your mailing and report back to you when the pieces were received at the seed address. It'll even comment on the condition of the piece. Or you can have it mail the seed pieces back to you so you can evaluate their condition yourself.

US Monitor will allow you to check the delivery status for each region you mail to. If you notice response rates seem low from some area, you can check the US Monitor report online and find out if any of your sales pieces have been delivered or not. For example, you may find that the mail has not reached the Northeast. Knowing this you can contact the post office to see what is going on.

The other tracking service I recommend is TrackMyMail.com. Rather than give you seed names, it actually puts a special barcode, called a planet code, on your sales piece. This barcode will be scanned by the USPS at each USPS location the mail passes through. This code will help track your mail piece, and you'll know when it's received by the closest post office to where the mail is delivered. If you are mailing to a small town in Montana, TrackMyMail.com will keep an eye on it until it reaches the city in Montana that you are mailing to.

TrackMyMail.com will not tell you how your pieces look, but it has great online tracking features so you can follow your mail as it's being delivered. This will give you peace of mind because you'll know your mail is moving and is being delivered.

Every Door Direct Mail—An Ideal Solution for the Local Business

Every Door Direct Mail is a program developed by the USPS to help more businesses benefit from direct mail. It allows you to blanket specific neighborhoods and is therefore great for regional businesses. For example, if you have a pizza shop and want to send an offer to everyone within a two-mile radius of your restaurant, Every Door Direct Mail will allow you to send out any size standard flat mail piece for an extremely low fee—about one-third the normal rate. The mail will be delivered to every address in that area. You don't need a postage permit or a list of names. And there is no annual fee. All you have to do is show up at your local post office and drop off your mail.

So if you have a regional business and want to contact everyone within a specific neighborhood, then Every Door Direct Mail is a great fit for you. However, there are a few drawbacks you should be aware of. The USPS allows you to mail to everyone only on a specific carrier route. You can't segment out some of the names or addresses for factors like age, income, or previous buying habits. You have to mail to everyone on the route, which can be a problem if your product or service has a limited group of buyers.

If you have a specific buyer in mind, Every Door Direct Mail is probably not your best option. But if you have a regional business that appeals to a broad audience, such as a restaurant, tire shop, car dealership, etc., and you want to reach every household or business in a limited area, this is a very cost-effective way to meet your goals.

Well, you're almost a mail expert now. But there's still one gap that needs to be filled in: the process of scheduling all the different parts of the operation.

There are a lot of steps in putting together your direct-mail campaign, and they have to fall into place like clockwork to get the best results. Chapter 12 will make you an expert on scheduling the entire production.

Why You Should Be an Information Marketer

By Dan S. Kennedy

O NE OF THE ESSENTIAL ELEMENTS OF A DIRECT-MAIL PIECE OR **package to elicit response is an offer**. In seeking response from new people, new prospects, and leads or first-time customers, the *nature* of the offer is critical. A common approach is the irresistible offer directly involving the goods or services of the marketer, often featuring a huge discount or even a free trial, exam, consultation, etc. A more interesting approach, far less hazardous to your price integrity, is the irresistible *information* offer.

A financial advisor client of mine, under my direction, switched her lead-generation advertising in print, on radio, and by direct mail to offering relevant, interesting information "widgets" (reports, book, CD, online video, etc.) in place of "call for appointment" or "attend my workshop." The results?

1. Fewer leads,
2. higher cost per lead . . .

BUT

3. higher conversion of prospects to clients,
4. better, more valuable clients,
5. more easily sold to and managed, and thus
6. more money from fewer clients and less work.

Direct mail is the perfect vehicle for offering information. Proof: The entire newsletter industry, a thriving, multibillion-dollar industry revolves around direct mail for securing new subscribers. Proof and important news: In almost every category where businesses sell products or services, there are excellent mailing lists of consumers who have paid to get information about that subject matter. If you own an organic grocery, there are lists of people who've paid for information about healthier eating and cooking. If you own a sporting goods store, there are lists of people who've paid for information about playing better golf, rock climbing, or running marathons. People who pay to get certain information are very likely to respond to an offer for interesting *free* information of the same nature. This is how you build a bridge on which a customer can walk to you and then buy and become a customer, rather than asking them to leap.

Direct mail does something interesting in the book business, too. In 2011 through 2012 there were over 200 books about diabetes published traditionally, for sale in bookstores, via Amazon, etc. Many were nearly dead on arrival, never even selling their small first printings. Fewer than 10% topped 15,000 copies sold. Average price: $10. In that same time period, a friend of mine sold over 200,000 copies of his diabetes book at about $50, at a profit, entirely and exclusively via direct mail, using the kinds of lists I described in Chapter 7. This is called Direct-to-Consumer Publishing. It bypasses all agents, editors, publishers, interference with the author, distribution, forced discounting, and, by showing up alone, all competition. And by creating a mailing list, it provides a basis for a business behind the book. This is but one example of thousands that prove people will respond to offers of relevant information about health offered via direct mail, and that should fascinate any dentist, chiropractor, medical doctor, psychologist, child psychologist, hospital administrator, etc.

There are similar examples in home improvement, gardening, fitness and exercise, weight loss, planning vacations, travel, investing, and hundreds more.

Yet, faced with these facts, the overwhelming majority of merchants, marketers, and professionals insist on advertising and selling their products or services instead of (first) offering information. The example of the diabetes book should tell every hospital executive and every doctor how to successfully use direct mail to attract top quality patients. But instead, most advertise and promote emergency rooms, having the number-two top-rated heart surgeon in Kansas, providing back-pain relief or dental implants, and so on. Opportunity is knocking, and they are stuffing cotton in their ears.

This is a perfect example of having profitable facts staring you in the face and refusing to acknowledge them, let alone capitalize on them.

Sad, really.

Even when it is clearly shown and explained to people, demonstrated with examples upon example, laid out bare, no secrets concealed, as I frequently do, businesspeople quite literally turn their back on it and return to their selling of their products or services just as they've been selling them all along. Despite declining results and diminishing returns, they ignore all just told to you here and every example shown to them.

The author of *Think And Grow Rich*, Napoleon Hill, cited "habit-force" as the most powerful of all forces, and I suppose he was right. People are blinded and made deaf, trapped and imprisoned, and intellectually retarded by their habits of thought and habitual ways of doing things. Just as I pull somebody out of their "like everybody else" advertising and selling of the cars or chiropractic care or whatever, their habit-force pulls them back in.

How to Break the Chains of Habit-Force and Escape the "Like Everybody Else" Prison

Maybe *you* are ready for a radical replacement of the "like everybody else" advertising and marketing rut. Some people, by the way, advertise and market like everybody else, but scream "Better." Others advertise and market like everybody else, but scream "Cheaper." Others advertise and market like everybody else, but try trickery: "This Weekend Only." But they are all still advertising and marketing like everybody else. IF *you* are ready for a radical replacement for the "like everybody else" advertising and marketing rut, *and you* actually follow through, break the chains of habit-force, and do something authentically different, know—and take pride in the fact—that you are the rarest of rare birds.

If you are such a bird, here is what to do.

- $ STOP advertising, marketing, and pitching your company, your products, your services, your prices, your sales event—whatever it is that you have habitually been pushing.
- $ CREATE relevant, appealing information and put it into an information "Widget" that your potential customers will want to get, have, find out about, and know.
- $ ONLY advertise, market, and promote that Widget. Nothing else. Just it.
- $ USE DIRECT MAIL to offer your Widget to the most qualified potential customers you can identify.

Then—and *only then*—after someone has stepped forward and asked for your information Widget, and you have used your Widget to demonstrate expertise, trustworthiness, and whatever other factors would make someone prefer to do business with you and rule out all other alternatives—may you invite the potential customer to a next step, leading to a sale. Until then, you may *not* wave your brand flag or cute logo or clever slogan. Until then, you may *not* even mention your product or service. Until then, you may *not* show your product, mention awards won, show your store or office, refer to price, or guarantee or any product features or benefits. You can *not* promise coupons or discounts.

If, for example, you own a fine restaurant and you plan to mail a letter to married men in your area two months in advance of their wedding anniversaries to offer them a free guide for "planning the most amazing anniversary date your wife has ever had and will never forget, for under $300," your letter *cannot* mention your restaurant, its views, its wine cellar, its five-star rating, its Kobe beef. None of that. Understand that habit force will tempt you to muck this up. This is an unfamiliar road less traveled. I get that. It involves what I teach as The Strategy of the Delayed Sale. You can find additional information about it and examples of it in my book *No B.S. Sales Success in the New Economy*, and in a book I co-authored with Chip Kessler, *Making Them Believe: The 21 Lost Marketing Secrets of Dr. J.R. Brinkley*.

If you are going to take this approach, and take it seriously, you will study actual information marketers in relevant categories—those selling books, courses, newsletters, etc., direct to consumers by direct mail (and other media as well). You will stop studying and copycatting your peers and trying to somehow advertise as they do but incrementally better. You will become an information marketer, with the only difference on the "back-end": where their back-end businesses are more books, subscriptions, seminars, etc., yours is a restaurant or a gym or a financial advisory service. But on the "front-end," you and they will be indistinguishable cousins. To get started, I suggest buying some books and subscribing to some newsletters from Direct to Consumer Publishers in your category. If you aren't on its mailing lists now, you can hack in through online media. Use search, find its sites, buy, subscribe. You'll quickly be on a mailing list rented to many mailers. Also, check out the Information Marketing Association at www.info-marketing.org.

200 $ THE DIRECT-MAIL SOLUTION

The Low-Threshold vs. High-Threshold Secret

In the book *Uncensored Sales Secrets* by Sydney Barrows, which I
contributed to, we introduce mall developer Arnold Taubman's concept
of "threshold resistance." In retail, he means it to describe how inviting
or how off-putting the front of a store or restaurant is and what can
be seen immediately inside it. He says many retailers set up too much
threshold resistance.

Many marketers do the same thing with the reason and means
of response they offer. High thresholds require a person to call,
knowing they will talk to a (dreaded) salesperson, or to come into
a store or showroom where she will be confronted by a (dreaded)
salesman. High thresholds make the response about buying the
product or service. One of the lowest thresholds is "let me send you
information about."

Elsewhere in this book, Craig talks to you about list segmentation.
I want you to understand that it is linked to the allocation of
financial resources. If you have, for example, $10,000.00 to invest,
you can spread it wide and thin, with outreach to 5,000 people at $2
each. Or to 500 people who are somehow known to be much more
interested, at $20 each. Or to just 100 known to be hyperinterested,
at $100 each. Clearly, the more invested in each prospect, the more
impact you can have. By first advancing a low-threshold offer, you
carve a segment out of a big list (or create a list from advertising
in other media) so that you can then invest in those who have
demonstrated interest.

In the book *Buy Now*, infomercial industry peers of mine, Rick
Cesari and Ron Lynch, explain the making of the multimillion-
dollar Juiceman-brand countertop juicer business this way. When
spokesperson Jay Kordich did thousands of radio interviews and
the breakthrough TV appearance on *The Today Show,* he didn't pitch
the juicer or offer literature about it. He offered free healthy-eating
recipes. People who took the trouble to write in and request those

CHAPTER 11 / WHY YOU SHOULD BE AN INFORMATION MARKETER

recipes identified themselves as very interested in healthier eating and curing health problems naturally. *Those* were the prospects to invest substantially in marketing to. They built their list with a low-threshold, perceived high-value, free offer of information.

If you would like to see the low-threshold offer used at GKIC, available to you as a test-drive of all the marketing resources and support offered, refer to Craig's GKIC affiliate site www.dankennedy.com/DirectMailSolution.

If You Are Going to Do Direct Mail, You'll Be Fighting for Response

Direct mail reveals—painfully—a truth about all advertising and marketing that a lot of other media hides: Only a tiny, tiny percentage of people give their attention to your advertising or marketing. Most ignore you. With a lot of ad media, you don't realize how much you are being ignored. But with direct mail we know. Because there's no ambiguity about the investment being made, we must fight for every response.

In the football movie *On Any Given Sunday*, the coach played by Al Pacino gives a locker room speech about *inches*. About fighting hard for each and every inch, for victory or defeat is not really the result of a dramatic big play that covers half the field. If such a play appears to win the game, it was made possible by winning the battle of inches, and it mattered because the battle of inches was won. Success in business in toto works the same way. Success with direct mail profoundly works this way. Each headline choice, each photo choice, each graphic choice, and each list choice matters even if it affects only one person per hundred reading it (the rough result of 10,000 getting it).

Your decisions about the height of the threshold and the amount of threshold resistance your offer engenders must be the best they can be. At times, you will want to discourage mass, poorly qualified response.

But know that the response you do get will have been fought for and hard won. Be careful not to ask too much of your direct mail or of your brand-new prospect or first-time customer, client, patient, or donor.

Putting It All Together—the Details of Scheduling a Direct-Mail Campaign

WHEN A GENERAL PLANS A MAJOR OPERATION, HE DRAWS UP A big schedule of what has to happen and when. Without that, it would be chaos in the field. Someone has to have the big picture and make sure everything happens when it's supposed to.

In the same way, a successful direct-mail campaign always begins with one very important step: strategically creating a direct-mail plan. Skipping the planning stage and jumping right into making decisions about the mailing will be a detriment to your campaign and your pocket book.

In the following pages I'm going to show you the exact planning process I use to create almost 300 direct-mail campaigns per year—beginning with a handy method that will help you define who you are and where you stand.

SWOT

A successful mail campaign has its foundation in a strong beginning. Many direct-mail companies start at the very beginning by using a direct-marketing analysis method called "SWOT" to create and plan a campaign. SWOT is a useful tool that will help you scrutinize all the critical aspects of your situation before you enter into the direct-mail stream.

SWOT stands for Strengths, Weaknesses, Opportunities, and Threats. Utilizing the SWOT analysis will help you focus your direct-mail campaign so that it's more targeted and efficient. In this way it will save you money, and by leading to a more effective campaign, it will add more money to your bank account.

The first SWOT action is to identify your strengths. What is it that you do or offer that no one else can or does? Do you have more experience? Have you been in business longer? Is your product superior? Do your customers give you great reviews and testimonials? Do you have a great reputation? Have you won awards? What makes you different and special?

Next you need to identify your weaknesses that could prevent you from reaching your marketing objectives. What do you need to improve on? Do you need to provide better customer service? Could you get better at tracking your campaigns? Are you losing out by not following up with your customers? Are you saddled with a tight budget? You can't deal properly with these issues until you've named them.

After you've identified some of your strengths and weaknesses, you need to take a close look at your opportunities. What direct-mail opportunities do you have right now? Have you just identified a targeted universe of prospects? Do you have a new product or service to offer? Are you able to offer special pricing? Maybe it's time for a Holiday Special—or perhaps an Inventory Blowout. What is going on right now that offers a unique opportunity to expand your customer base and build sales?

The last part of SWOT that you need to look at has to do with potential threats. What "threats" could hinder your marketing campaign? Perhaps it's a direct competitor in your niche/market— perhaps a company that has a very similar offer to yours. Or perhaps it's a timing issue. Is this the right time to make your offer?

This SWOT exercise will help you identify the areas that you need to focus on in your direct-mail campaigns and the limitations within your organization that you have to learn to overcome or work within. In essence, you want to use what you learn to:

- Target your Strengths
- Fix your Weaknesses
- Identify your Opportunities
- Reduce the Threats that could negatively impact your campaign

Once you have gone through the SWOT exercise and addressed the issues it raises, you will know what your offer should be, who your target audience is, and what kind of package you should mail out to best meet your goals. Now you can start planning the rest of the details of your direct-mail campaign.

Steps of a Direct-Mail Campaign

There are many details that go into setting up a mail campaign. The task can sometimes seem enormous and overwhelming—especially when it's all new to you. However, once you get organized, you'll see it's not that difficult. If you establish a set of procedures to follow for each mailing and use a checklist to guide you, scheduling your campaign can be much faster and easier than you suspect it will be.

There are a few things that must be taken care of before you select your mailing date.

- Write the sales copy.
- Get the sales piece designed.
- Select the vendors you'll use.

I can't count the number of campaigns I've worked on where the client insisted that I order mailing lists and schedule the campaign before the copy and design were finished. Nine times out of 10 the copy wasn't completed in time, and we had to put the mailing on hold until the company could finish it up. Sometimes the delay put us six or eight weeks behind schedule.

This kind of poor planning can cause you to rush your sales copy just to meet a printing deadline or a specific mail date. This is when costly errors in the copy and critical design flaws can creep in.

Not only that, if you order your list too soon, and your list broker provides the names on time, but you're not ready to use them, the lists could sit around for a couple of months untouched. Every day the names get older, people may move, interests may change, and the targeted list you paid so much money for could lose a great deal of its value before you can use it. It's better to have the sales piece finished and ready to go to the printer before you completely schedule your mail campaign.

I once had a client give me the sales piece, saying everything was "100 percent finished, double-checked, and ready to go." After reviewing the sales piece and double-checking it myself, I found out the client had put in a new 800 number, but the number had not been transferred to its phone system yet. We caught it in time, but you can imagine the detriment that would have been to the campaign if the phone number had not been corrected.

It is very important that you spend the time needed to make sure your sales copy is checked and double-checked. Chapter 2 has more details on how to write sales copy that makes the cash register ring. Writing great copy is one thing—but making sure all the details are accurate is also critical.

Once you have your sales copy and design finished, you need to select the printer, mailing facility, and data-processing company you will use. Make sure you have references from each of these companies prior to making your final selection—and check them out!

You'll want to get quotes from three different vendors to ensure that you are getting the best pricing. This is tough to do if you are working under a tight deadline. Allow yourself some time so you can negotiate the best price between a few different vendors.

Knowing in advance which vendor you are going to use for each step of the process will give you peace of mind as your mail date approaches. Scrambling at the last minute rarely brings the best results.

How Long Will It Take to Get a Mailing Ready and into the Mail Stream?

It all depends on how many pieces you're mailing, how complicated the sales package is that you're putting together, how big your mailing lists are, and what type of list you're mailing to

The List

If you're mailing to your own house file, names that you already have, and it's only a few hundred, you could get your list ready within a day. If it's thousands, you could get it out in a couple of days. If you're renting lists, you're having to do a merge purge, and your sales pieces are being printed in another location, it could take a couple of weeks to get it all together. If you are printing hundreds of thousands of pieces and renting dozens of mailing lists, it could take up to a month.

The Package

If the package is simple, like a short sales letter, you can get it into the mail quickly. If you're sending dimensional mail, it will take more time to put the package together. For example, if you are mailing a message in a bottle, then you'll have to get the bottles, print the message, and have it inserted into the bottle. This will obviously take a lot longer to get into the mail.

You can start scheduling your mail campaigns once your sales piece is finished and you know which vendors you are going to use. Normally, you can plan to mail two to four weeks from the time you place your list orders. The length of time needed to prepare your mail campaign will depend on the number of names being mailed and how quickly your vendors can complete your job. If you're only mailing to a few thousand names, you probably can get the mail out in a week or two. But, if you are mailing a million pieces, you'll most likely need four weeks to complete all the necessary preparations.

Printing for more than one campaign at a time can shorten the lead time needed to get your sales pieces in the mail the next time (and it will save you money!). If you have a control sales piece that you know you are going to use in more than one mail campaign, consider printing enough extra pieces to cover the next mailing or two. This will give you extra pieces on hand so the next time you are ready to do a mailing, you will not have to wait for the printer to print and bind/insert your sales material. But, if you think you may be making a change to the sales piece, don't plan on printing extra sales pieces. They will just go to waste.

Figure 12–1 is a basic schedule I've used thousands of times to put together mail campaigns with the aim of acquiring new customers or leads. (Note: This schedule is based on a four-week schedule.)

You can download a sample of this schedule at www.TheDirect MailSolution.com.

Here are the details for each item in the mailing checklist.

Note: Most of these areas have been covered in detail in other sections of this book.

Write Sales Copy and Sales Copy Design

Don't get caught in scheduling problems. Make sure your piece is written and laid out before scheduling the rest of your mail campaign.

Give List Broker the Mail Schedule

Plan ahead with your list broker, and make sure your broker is aware of your mailing schedule. You'll want your broker to make several list

FIGURE 12-1 Direct Mail Schedule and Checklist

Direct Mail Schedule and Checklist
4 Week Leadtime

☐	Write Sales Copy for Your Offer	Must Be Done Prior To Scheduling Out Direct Mail Campaign	Date: _____
☐	Sales Copy Design - Lay Out the Sales Piece in the Format You Want to Mail		Date: _____
☐	Give List Broker the Mail Schedule & Ask For List Recommendations	32 Days Prior To Mail Date	Date: _____
☐	Request Printing Quote for Sales Piece	32 Days Prior To Mail Date	Date: _____
☐	Place List Orders with List Broker	28 Days Prior To Mail Date	Date: _____
☐	Give Mailing Schedule to Data Processing Company	25 Days Prior To Mail Date	Date: _____
☐	Artwork Due at Printer	25 Days Prior To Mail Date	Date: _____
☐	Approve Bluelines and Color Proof From Printer	22 Days Prior To Mail Date	Date: _____
☐	Send Data Processor Suppression Files and Seed List	15 Days Prior To Mail Date	Date: _____
☐	List Due Date	14 Days Prior To Mail Date	Date: _____
☐	Issue Merge Purge Instructions	14 Days Prior To Mail Date	Date: _____
☐	Approve Merge Purge	11 Days Prior To Mail Date	Date: _____
☐	Issue Key Codes and Splits	11 Days Prior To Mail Date	Date: _____
☐	Issue Lettershop Instructions	11 Days Prior To Mail Date	Date: _____
☐	Approve Key Codes and Splits	10 Days Prior To Mail Date	Date: _____
☐	Mail File Due at Lettershop	7 Days Prior To Mail Date	Date: _____
☐	Printing Due at Lettershop	7 Days Prior To Mail Date	Date: _____
☐	Postage Request from Lettershop	3 Days Prior To Mail Date	Date: _____
☐	Approve Address Panel(s)	3 Days Prior To Mail Date	Date: _____
☐	Special Reports Due From Data Processor (Broker Report, Net Name Report, Interaction Report)	2 Days Prior To Mail Date	Date: _____
☐	Postage Due	1 Day Prior To Mail Date	Date: _____

Mail Date:

recommendations, and the more time you allow for the process, the more research he or she will be able to do. Provide your broker with a copy of the sales piece you are mailing and, if possible, a copy of the product you are selling. By doing these things you will help your broker recommend the best lists for you. Normally, I like to give the broker at least four days' notice if it's a product or service I've mailed before. If it's a new product or service, I like to give the broker at least two weeks.

Request Printing Quote for Sales Piece

Get price quotes from several different printers. Select the printer who offers the best combination of price and service.

Place List Orders with Broker

After you've selected the lists you want to mail, it's time to place an order with your list broker. Tell your broker what the list due date is and where you want the lists to go. You have several options for where to have the mailing lists sent.

1. You can send directly to your printer or mailing facility. Make sure it has the software to perform the merge purge, data hygiene, and NCOA.
2. Larger mailings require a data-processing company that can better handle jobs that are more complicated (more lists, more variables to consider).
3. Many list brokers offer a data-processing service.

When placing your list orders, assign each list an order number, or you can use the broker's order number. This will help the data processing company know what the lists are when they receive the files.

Also ask your list broker to send back an order confirmation—it's always good to document everything.

Give Mailing Schedule to Data-Processing Company

The company that is going to handle your merge purge and data hygiene will need to know when the list due date is—i.e., the date that all the rented lists should be in. It will also need to know what lists you ordered and their order numbers. This will help it identify which lists it's received and whether any are missing. You'll want the data-processing company to give you an update every day so that you and your broker can keep an eye on which lists have come in.

You'll also want to give the data processor instructions concerning what type of data hygiene you want to use. That way, once all the lists are in, it knows exactly what's needed to clean up your lists.

Artwork Due at Printer

This is the date on which you need to have the file containing your sales piece at the print shop. Have the print shop tell you how much lead time it needs in order to get your job done on time, and make sure you send the file in a format the printer can read. Each printer works off a different schedule and uses different computer programs. Confirming this information in advance will save you time and money.

Approve Bluelines and Color Proof from Printer

After the print shop receives your file, it will output a blueline and color proof—or email a PDF. The blueline is taken directly from the film that will be used to create printing plates. On the blueline, you need to check the copy, line breaks, page breaks, borders, cropping—in other words, everything. This is your last chance to make changes. But be aware the printer may charge you for every change, so make sure you do a very good proof on the piece before you get to this stage. And for the color proof, check the colors on the proof to make sure they are exactly what you want to use in your sales piece. Make sure there are no errors. Any errors found on the blueline will end up on your printed material unless you make the correction. Again, most printers will charge you for changes that are not their fault, since they have to make the change and then output new film and a new set of proofs for you to review.

It's becoming more and more common for printers to just send a PDF proof via email. This method is adequate for small jobs, but I would suggest using the blueline and color proof for all large printing jobs.

Send Data Processor Suppression Files and Seed List

The suppression files are names you want to omit from the mailing. For example, if you are mailing an offer to sell a limited edition watch, you will want to omit all prior buyers of that watch. You wouldn't want to mail to someone who has already purchased the product you are offering. This "suppression file" may also be called a "customer file," "customer-suppression file," or "house file."

The decoy or seed list is the group of names and addresses you use to track delivery of the mailing. If the mailing is going out from the Los Angeles post office, you will want to know when your mail is delivered in different places across the nation. The "seed list" would have the names of individuals in different regions of the country who will inform you when they receive the sales piece and let you know what condition the piece is in when it arrives. You can subscribe to a service that provides seed names and addresses. I recommend US Monitor or TrackMyMail.com.

Mailing List Due Date

This is the date all the lists are due at the data processor. Normally the lists come in before the due date, but if a list is not in by this date, you'll need to cancel it. You don't want to hold up the merge purge and possibly risk changing the mail date over one list not arriving on time.

Prior to the list due date, keep track of the lists as they arrive at the data-processing company. Check the number of names the list owner sent and compare it with the number of names you ordered. If you ordered 10,000 names and the list owner shipped 20,000—find out why. The list owner may have pulled the wrong file or made a mistake in your order. Maybe you specified that you want to mail only to men over 50, and the list owner accidentally sent the entire file. You'll obviously want them to resend the file if they made a mistake.

Issue Merge Purge Instructions and
Approve Merge Purge

These are the instructions you give to the data processor indicating what criteria you want to use for running the merge. After the merge purge is completed, check over the results to see if there are any red flags. For example, if after the merge purge one of your 10,000-name lists is reduced to 2,000 names, you should probably investigate why.

Issue Key Codes and Splits

The key codes are used to track the effectiveness of different elements of your campaign, such as lists, copy variations, sales package, etc. These codes will help you know what the response rate is for each list, and they'll tell you how well your test pieces are doing.

Issue Lettershop Instructions

These instructions tell the lettershop—the company assembling your mail pieces and preparing the mailing for the post office—how to process your job. I like to give these instructions before the mail file even arrives. That way it can be prepared, and it'll know exactly what to do once your file comes in.

Tell them:

- $ Where the address label should appear on your sales piece
- $ What type of font you want for imprinting the address information
- $ What class of mail you want to use—first class or standard/bulk
- $ If you are mailing a letter package, specify the insertion order for each component and in what direction you want everything to face

Ask the lettershop to presort the mail file. Presorting your mail file into mail groups by ZIP codes will save the Postal Service time, and it will give you a discount for doing some of the work. If your mailing is large enough, you can ship it directly to the Postal Service bulk mail centers and save even more on postage costs.

Bulk mailing isn't the only way to save money. You can also presort first-class mail and receive discounts from the Postal Service.

Some printers have a mailing facility or lettershop in-house. This will save on the time it would take to ship the printed material to an off-site lettershop.

Keep in mind that the lettershop is the last contact you will have with your mail campaign. After your mail is dropped off at the post office, it's completely out of your hands.

Approve Key Codes and Splits

After you've given the data processor your key codes and splits, it should send back a confirmation and sample. The data processor needs to apply the instructions you gave it and then let you approve. If you are mailing 50 lists, and each list is broken up into three splits (tests), that's 150 different key codes. These key codes are vital to effectively tracking your mail campaign. There is no room for error here. This step is very important. First, assign key codes for tracking, and then make sure to double-check and approve them!

Mail File Due at Lettershop

This is the date the data processor needs the final mail file at the lettershop.

Printing Due at Lettershop

Your sales material is due at the lettershop on the same day that the mail file is due. The lettershop will then have everything needed to start processing your job.

Postage Request from Lettershop

The lettershop will take your mail file and calculate the total postage for your mailing. Then, it'll send you a request for postage. You'll need to get a check to the lettershop ASAP. The Postal Service will not accept your mailing unless the postage is paid in advance.

Some companies set up a mailing permit with the Postal Service. By doing this, you can keep a running account with money in it so you'll always be ready for your next mail campaign. That would save you from having to overnight a check to the lettershop.

Approve Address Panel(s)

When the mail file is ready to be ink-jetted on your sales piece or printed on a label, ask the mailing facility to fax or email you a sample of how the name and address will appear. Check to see that everything looks exactly the way you want it to, and that it appears in the correct place on the sales material. If it's printed in the wrong place or the font is hard to read, your mailing response rate could be lowered. It's easy for the lettershop to get the sample to you, and it will help ensure that no mistakes are made.

Reports Due from Data Processor

After the merge purge is complete, the data processor will send you reports from the merge purge process. You'll want to review these reports and then, if necessary, send portions of them to your list broker so you can get the deductions you deserve on your list rental.

A mail campaign is not complete without submitting verification for discounts. You always want to get as many discounts as possible because it affects your profit potential on the mailing. If you are using a data-processing company, ask it for an "interaction report" or "match analysis report" and "broker report" (it may call it something different).

An interaction report will show you how lists duplicated with one another, how your suppression file duplicated with the rented lists, and how other suppression files (like a prison suppression file or deceased file) impacted the merge.

A broker report is basically a report for the list broker that shows how many names you should be billed for on each list. This report will

> ## *Reminder*
>
> The DMA pander file is a list from the Direct Mail Association of people who have asked NOT to receive sales information in the mail. It is essential to suppress these names out of all prospect mailings. It will most likely make these people mad if they get mail from you. They may even call and complain.
>
> I once had a client who included a business reply envelope with its sales letter. One prospect taped the envelope to a red brick and mailed it back. The USPS actually delivered it back to my client. The USPS ended up not charging the client for return postage, but you would think it would have tossed it out or not accepted it in the first place. In any event, it was a good lesson learned.

show how many names had bad ZIP codes, intra duplicates (duplicate names within a list), deceased names, DMA pander names, etc.

The broker report and interaction report will reveal all the discounts available. These discounts will add up. You'll need to work with your list broker and data processor to create reports that work for everyone.

Postage Due Date

It is necessary that you have the postage due to the lettershop the day before the mailing. You don't want to miss your mail date because you didn't get your postage in on time.

After your mailing has been dropped off at the post office, get a verification form confirming the number of pieces it received from you, the class of mail, and the total cost. The copy of the Postal Service form should be signed by a Postal Service employee. If possible, you also want the form to have the Postal Service "date stamp" for the day your mail entered the mail stream. This verification will inform you whether or not the lettershop mailed the correct number of pieces and on the correct day

Now You Have All the Facts You Need to Start Planning a Direct-Mail Campaign

This book has given you all the information you need to plan and direct a successful direct-mail campaign. This means you are ready to use proven, time-tested methods to build your customer base. I hope you will use this knowledge to multiply your business many times over!

We've covered a great deal of material. Use this book as a reference that you return to as you go through the planning stages of your future campaigns. I've also put together a website that has sample sales pieces, a downloadable mailing schedule, sample spreadsheets, and much more! Go to www.TheDirectMailSolution.com.

People have made millions of dollars using direct-mail marketing. I know that for a fact, because I've directed their campaigns and I've seen it happen over and over.

Now you have everything you can use to make direct mail a success for your business too!

About the Authors

CRAIG SIMPSON IS THE OWNER OF SIMPSON DIRECT INC., A direct-marketing firm based in Grants Pass, Oregon. Since beginning his career in direct mail nearly 20 years ago, he has managed thousands of direct-mail campaigns, helping to gross hundreds of millions in revenue for his clients.

His direct-marketing company sends out nearly 300 mailings per year for his private clients. He works in practically every industry, marketing everything from courses on the benefits of drinking water to technical software, retail stores, real estate investment, financial services, health products, diet programs, insurance, and even wholesale clothing.

Craig's knowledge of list management and direct-marketing techniques has earned him the title of the nation's leading expert in direct-mail marketing. He is regularly asked to speak at national events on his experience with direct mail. He is the author of *The Direct-Mail Solution,* co-written with Dan Kennedy, available from EntrepreneurBookstore.com.

DAN S. KENNEDY is a multimillionaire serial entrepreneur, strategic advisor, and consultant, and one of the highest paid direct-response copywriters in the world. As an author, speaker, and coach, he directly influences over one million business owners annually. Information about his books can be found at www.NoBSBooks.com. Direct contact with Dan's office: fax 602-269-3113.

Other Books by Dan S. Kennedy

In the No B.S. series, published by Entrepreneur Press

> *No B.S. Guide to DIRECT Marketing for NON-Direct Marketing Businesses* (2nd Ed.)

> *No B.S. Guide to Marketing to Leading-Edge Boomers and Seniors* (with Chip Kessler)

> *No B.S. Guide to Trust-Based Marketing* (with Matt Zagula)

> *No B.S. Price Strategy* (with Jason Marrs)

> *No B.S. Guide to Marketing to the Affluent*

> *No B.S. BUSINESS Success in the New Economy*

> *No B.S. SALES Success in the New Economy*

> *No B.S. Wealth Attraction in the New Economy*

> *No B.S. Guide to Ruthless Management of People and Profits*

> *No B.S. Time Management for Entrepreneurs*

With other publishers:

> *Ultimate Sales Letter* (4th Edition—20th Anniversary Edition)
> *Ultimate Marketing Plan* (4th Edition—20th Anniversary Edition)
> *Making Them Believe: The 21 Lost Secrets of Dr. Brinkley-Style Marketing* (with Chip Kessler)

The New Psycho-Cybernetics (with Dr. Maxwell Maltz)
Unfinished Business/Autobiographical Essays
Make 'Em Laugh & Take Their Money

BOOKS CONTRIBUTED TO

Uncensored Sales Strategies by Sydney Barrow with Dan Kennedy
Marketing Miracles
Win, Place or Die: A Mystery Novel by Les Roberts with Dan Kennedy

Index